Robert Hamilton

Remarks on the means of obviating the fatal effects of the bite of a

mad dog,

Or other rabid animal: with observations on the method of cure when hydrophobia

occurs: and the opinion relative to worming of dogs refuted : illustrated by

examples

Robert Hamilton

Remarks on the means of obviating the fatal effects of the bite of a mad dog,
Or other rabid animal: with observations on the method of cure when hydrophobia occurs:
and the opinion relative to worming of dogs refuted : illustrated by examples

ISBN/EAN: 9783337814946

Printed in Europe, USA, Canada, Australia, Japan

Cover: Foto ©ninafisch / pixelio.de

More available books at **www.hansebooks.com**

REMARKS

ON THE

Means of obviating the fatal Effects

OF THE

BITE of a MAD DOG,

Or other rabid Animal;

WITH

OBSERVATIONS

ON THE

Method of Cure when Hydrophobia occurs;

AND THE

Opinion relative to Worming of Dogs refuted.

ILLUSTRATED BY EXAMPLES.

———————

By R. HAMILTON, M. D.

Of the Royal College of Phyſicians in London, and Member of the Medical, Phyſical, and other Literary Societies in Edinburgh and London.

———————

MORSU VIRUS HABENT, ET FATUM DENTE MINANTUR.
LUCAN. PHARSAL.
ALIORUM FACTIS, NOBIS QUOD EX USU SIT ADMONEMUR.
CRATO.

IPSWICH:

PRINTED BY SHAVE AND JACKSON.
SOLD BY J. SHAVE, IPSWICH; T. LONGMAN, PATER-NOS-
TER-ROW, LONDON; AND BY ALL THE BOOKSELLERS
IN SUFFOLK, NORFOLK, AND ESSEX.
MDCCLXXXV.

TO

WILLIAM HAMILTON, Esq. M. D.

Physician to the Surrey Dispensary, London,

THE FOLLOWING PAGES ARE GRATEFULLY INSCRIBED,

As an Expreffion of unfeigned Efteem,

AND OF

The Senfe retained of his Friendfhip,

By his obedient, and obliged

Humble Servant,

The AUTHOR.

PREFACE.

IN consequence of an accident from the bite of a mad dog having lately happened, whereby a young gentleman of a respectable family in the county of Suffolk lost his life,* a few observations on the means of preventing Hydrophobia were then inserted in the Ipswich Journal for the perusal of the neighbourhood, to enable them, in some measure, to oppose the fatal effects of the bite of a rabid animal, should the like happen among them in future.

THOUGH

* Son of Admiral Rowley.

THOUGH drawn up in haste, and published incorrectly, yet they were read, and, in general, met with approbation ; but, as the limits of a newspaper confined them to a very narrow compass, and forbade a more minute discussion, the author, who was soon discovered, was solicited by several gentlemen to enter more fully into the subject, and lay them before the public in form of a pamphlet.

WITH this he complied, yet not without hesitation, when he considered how many eminent men had trod the same path before him, whom he knew, he must be contented, *passibus inæqualibus*, to follow

follow at an humble diſtance, in-
ſtead of expecting to ſurpaſs.

THOUGH the partiality of friends
flattered him his remarks would be
acceptable, yet the taſk was not
undertaken from a preſumption of
his being able to convey much information, or throw more light on
the ſubject than what authors had
already done, but ſolely with a deſire to be uſeful, as far as he was
able, to that part of the commu-
nity eſpecially with which he was
now more immediately connected,
among whom the recent misfortune
had ſpread conſiderable alarm.

BEYOND the limits of a pamphlet, at firſt, and a ſhort one too,

it

it was not his intention to lengthen thefe pages ; but, in purfuing his plan, it was found impoffible to furnifh even a well digefted outline, much lefs difcufs the fubjeɗ with any degree of perfpicuity, within fo narrow a compafs ; hence it be-came incumbent on him to extend them.

HE has ventured throughout to deliver his fentiments freely, though with deference, and as freely canvaffed thofe of men much his fuperiors in abilities, and confequence in the fcale of fcience. For this, he hopes, however, the public will acquit him, by allowing him a right to offer his opinion, provided it be done with becoming modefty.

Here,

Here, indeed, *they*, not *he*, muft judge; and he trufts, he fhall not be found, in the following pages, to have tranfgreffed in this refpect.

He has collected obfervations from the works of authors both antient and modern, and endeavoured, as far as he was able, to diftinguifh between what could be fupported on the grounds of rational induction, and what had only (as appeared to him) fuperftition and credulity to lean on.

This effay is not offered to the public as perfect. Far from it. The author is too confcious of its imperfection. Yet he hopes it will be found to contain, at leaft, an

b   out-

outline of what is known on the
fubject. Hints, perhaps, may be
gathered from it, as materials for
men of greater abilities to work
with, who may hereafter turn their
attention to its farther inveftigation.
With this view he fubjects himfelf
to the public tribunal, not doubt-
ing to meet with clemency; but
that it will, at leaft, correct with
lenity, where the candour of cri-
ticifm cannot beftow approbation.

HE would here alfo beg leave to
offer his thanks to thofe gentlemen
who favoured him with communi-
cations, and for the public ufe feveral of them fo readily allowed
him to make of their remarks.
Among others, he holds himfelf
                              parti-

particularly obliged to the ingenious and indefatigable Mr. John Hunter, who not only honoured him with frequent correfpondence, but, with a liberality of mind, allowed him a public ufe of the information conveyed, with the fanction of his name to corroborate it, a name which every cultivator of medical fcience muft long hold in efteem. To Sir Thomas Gooch, Bart. he likewife returns thanks for the honour he conferred by his letters, and the fatisfaction his anfwers afforded to fome enquiries made by the author on the fubject.

REMARKS

REMARKS

On the Means of obviating the fatal Effects of the BITE *of a* MAD DOG, *or other rabid Animal,* &c.

MANY authors, of refpectable abili-ties, have attempted to inveftigate the nature of the difeafe occafioned by the poifon from the bite of a mad animal. Much has been wrote, and various remedies propofed, almoft from the earlieft annals of the ftudy of difeafes; yet it ftill remains,

in

in a great meafure, the reproach of the
medical profeffion.

PROPHYLACTIC means, however, are in
our power; for though we have hitherto
failed in our attempts to cure the Hydrophobia, as it is generally called, though
perhaps with fome impropriety, or that
fpafmodic affection of the organs of deglutition, which, for the moft part, take place,
yet, by timely care and perfeverance, we
may, I am perfuaded, with tolerable certainty, obviate it.

THE firft queftion that naturally occurs
here, is, What are the figns by which we
can difcover the firft ftage of madnefs in
the canine tribe ? This feems a neceffary
inquiry, fince many are fo ignorant on this
fubject as to rufh precipitately on their own
ruin, either by attempting to fondle, or
fhew marks of rafh kindnefs to dogs almoft
in the laft ftage of their illnefs.

THE

THE dog is an animal that, in a particular manner, attaches himfelf to man. He forfakes his own tribe, and adheres, with a ftrict fidelity to his mafter. This gives an opportunity for our obfervations. Thofe much accuftomed to this animal, can tell when he is difordered, from obferving his manner now and before this, and comparing them, with as much eafe as they can when any of their family are indifpofed. In the early ftage, however, it is not fo eafy to diftinguifh it with certainty from other difeafes, as it has feveral fymptoms in common with them. We find this the fame, indeed, in feveral of thofe incident to the human body. In the firft day, the fever that precedes the irruption of the meafles or fmall-pox, it is a difficult matter to fay with precifion, what it is, except from the prefumptive proof of one or other of thefe difeafes being frequent in the place. A little time longer, however, puts this beyond a doubt; we then obferve fome fymptoms peculiar to the refpective

difeafe

difeafe with which the individual is affected.
The fame may be faid of madnefs in dogs.

We fhall mention, neverthelefs, the following, as thofe which both obfervation
and the authority of the beft authors allow
to be founded in fact. :—1. A difinclination
for his food : he does not, it is true, refufe
it, but he takes it with an evident indiffer-
ence and liftleffnefs.   2. He is melancholy.
It is as eafy to mark this fymptom in the
dog, as in the human fpecies.   In health
he is frolickfome and playful ; but now he
hangs his tail, and, at the approach of his
mafter, or any other members of the family,
fhews none of that joy with which he was
wont to welcome them at their return
home.   3. His eyes appear mixed, and lefs
clear than formerly.   This may be called
the firft ftage ; yet there is fcarce any thing
pathognomonic here.

The fecond is more diftinctly marked:
for in a day or two more he refufes both

meat

meat and drink; ſhuns other dogs, and is equally ſhunned by them. Lo! here, the wiſdom of the Creator, who has endowed theſe animals, commonly called irrational, with an inſtinctive knowledge for their own preſervation. Obſervation, I think, does not prove they ſhun one another in other diſeaſes, to which, in common with other animals, they are liable.

Now comes the laſt ſtage: he quits the houſe; runs forward, he knows not where, or without any particular deſign; ſnaps, in his fury, or, perhaps, through the pain he ſuffers, at every animal that comes in his way; and, in the ſpace of two days after, or perhaps leſs, dies convulſed.

Such is the common progreſs of his ſufferings: and ſuch ſymptoms, we think, will be found invariable. Many others, indeed, might be added, as related by thoſe who have treated more amply on the ſub-ject,

ject, but thefe may be fufficient to diftinguifh the difeafe.

FROM this view of the ftages of the
malady it will appear, that a very little
attention might prevent any accident from
his bite : for, in the early ftage of his illnefs, when he only lowers and feems heavy,
he fhews almoft no marks of a change in
his temper ; he neither fnaps, nor bites at
any perfon near him ; and hence, in du-
bious cafes, where prudence raifes fufpicions, he might be eafily tied up, till time
fhould determine the event. Nor would
this be found long ; for, perhaps, lefs than
ten days may bring the whole fcene to a
conclufion, or fufficiently convince us that
our fears were groundlefs.

BUT fuppofe, now, that this has been
neglected ; or that the rabid animal has
unexpectedly come in the way, and unhap-
pily exercifed his fury, too fuccefsfully, on
one of the human fpecies : what then is to
be

be done?—As I am not writing for the information of the faculty, but for the utility and fafety of my neighbours, and common readers in general, who may think it worth their pains to perufe this fhort effay, it may be neceffary to inform them, that by the fuccefsful, though elaborate refearches of anatomifts, a fet of veffels have been difcovered in the bodies of animals, as well human, as others, of the higheft importance in their œconomy, called *Lacteals*; fometimes, nay, indeed, more commonly, *Lymphatics*, from the colour of their contents ; and poffeffing fome peculiarities not neceffary here to be mentioned.

THESE are difperfed plentifully over every part, as well external as internal. Their ufes are to feparate the nutritious parts of our aliment from the feculencies with which it is united, when taken into the ftomach, and convey it to the blood, where it is again farther elaborated into flefh, bone, cartilage, tendon, ligament, &c. by the different or-

gans

gans adapted by nature for making thefe new combinations. They drink up, in like manner, the fupurfluous lymph left in cavities, and other parts, where it had been depofited by another order of veffels, named likewife from their offices, *Exhalents*, and brought hither by them for feveral ufeful purpofes of nature; among others, for defending the more folid parts from too much friction on one another.

As we cannot wound the fmalleft part of the fkin without opening fome of thefe, whatever comes in their way, fo minute as to circulate in them, is drunk up, or, in the language of anatomifts, abforbed, and carried, by the affiftance of innumerable valves with which they are furnifhed, onwards with the reft of their contents to the general receptacle, or duct, where they all unite, forming a large canal, which ends under the clavicle on the left fide, where it is inferted into a large vein (the Subclavian

vian) that empties itfelf into the heart, mixing its contents with the whole mafs.

It is by the intervention of thefe we can ingraft difeafes, fuch as the fmall-pox; it is by thefe the venereal poifon, that juft tax on illicit pleafures, is received, contaminating the body, and enfeebling the conftitution; and by the intervention of thefe, the fatal poifon in the faliva of rabid animals is conveyed to the organs of life.

From this fhort fketch of the offices of thefe veffels, fo curioufly and wonderfully adapted for their purpofes by the Author of our being, it will readily appear, that if we can intercept their contents in their paffage to the heart, the effects, whatever they may be, whether for nourifhment, or for communicating poifons, and the feeds of difeafes, muft be prevented. Here, then, we have found a clue to guide our way: here, then, reafon bids us commence our work.

C   It

IT is no eafy tafk to determine, *à priore,* how foon this poifon may get beyond our reach. This depends on a variety of cir-cumftances. Among others, on the ftate of the habit at the time, to receive it; but chiefly, perhaps, on the nature of the poifon itfelf.

WE find from experience, which is here an unerring guide, that different poifons require different lengths of time to exert their force; but thefe periods, allowing fome variation for different habits of body, are found pretty regular with refpect to the fame poifon. Thus, the fmall-pox, for the moft part, appear from the eighth to the tenth day after inoculation; the poifon ab-forbed from unclean embraces has likewife its period, allowing, as above, for the ftate of the body at the time it is applied; and the fame may be faid of the poifon from a rabid animal (I mean the dog) which, ge-nerally fpeaking, appear about the fifth or

fixth

fixth week : fome, however, which I would call anamolous, or irregular cafes, have gone to as many months, before they difcovered themfelves by their effects ; but we recollect no well authenticated cafes where years have intervened.

To thefe poifons, too, under different circumftances, we may allow different degrees of virulence; which, united to the ftate of the body, and the peculiar idiofyncracy, or conftitution, may affift in forming the variations we obferve relative to the propagation of their refpective difeafes. There is a period of the fmall-pox which is found more infectious than another, as is well known to thofe accuftomed to ingraft the difeafe : matter taken from a puftule at this time more certainly communicates its effects. There is a time, perhaps, likewife, when the faliva of an infected dog is tainted with a higher degree of virulency, and this would appear to be, from the hiftories of cafes, the third, or laft ftage. It

is

is then the vifcid flaver is fecreted in largeft quantities; throwing the infected organs into more inordinate and preternatural actions.

To prove that the virus is abforbed in the manner we have endeavoured to def-cribe above, we need only, fome days after inoculating the variolous matter, cut out the part, and no fmall-pox fhall appear; no fever fhall be excited in the fyftem: it is nothing now but a local complaint, uncon-nected with the habit at large. Experiments have been inftituted for this end, and the event has correfponded with the doctrine of abforption. It is difficult, however, to fay, exactly, at what time after inoculation this can effectually be done, becaufe abforption takes place fooner or later from the varieties, and peculiarities of temparament, &c. al-ready hinted at.

We frequently find the patient, fome time before, or about the eighth day, com-plain of a pain in the courfe of the lym-phatics,

phatics, and in the axilla, of the the inoculated arm; or, if it be in the leg, in the
courfe of the thigh, and in the groin, where
we know lymphatics, and lymphatic glands
lie. The fame may be obferved of the venereal difeafe; and the fame remark has
been noted in the abforption of the poifon
from rabid animals.

THOUGH this conftantly precedes the fe-
brile fymptoms in the one, or the peculiar
fymptoms that conftitute the other relative
difeafes, yet, were we to make our experiment now, it would not be decifive; it
would not prevent the progrefs of the malady: for, enough of the poifon having got
beyond the reach of the knife, to propagate
the refpective difeafe, our taking away what
might remain in the part where it was firft
inferted, would not anfwer the end in view.
Our experiment here would fail, and it
would prove nothing. But when this is
done at an early time, when, from the inflamed appearance of the little fcar, we
might

might with certainty conclude the difeafe would be communicated, we may reft af-ufred our experiment fhall be decifive.

WHETHER the poifon of the mad dog multiplies itfelf by a fort of fermentative, or affimilating procefs, as fome of the lateft and beft writers affert of the variolous mat-ter, and that abforption does not take place, to infect the fyftem, till after this new com-bination is effected, is too obfcure a quef-tion to enter into here; nor would the readers for whom this fhort tract is chiefly drawn up, profit from the difcuffion.

IF this be allowed, however, we may be enabled to prevent the difeafe at a later period than we fhall venture to recommend by the means we are about to mention. But, fhould accident prevent us from put-ting thofe means in practice, which we fhall by and by call effectual, it will give a chance, and fome, though flender, grounds for hope.

THE

THE girl that was brought to the Edinburgh Royal Infirmary, in 1765, had her arm feared with a hot iron over the fcar where fhe received the bite, as foon as fhe was examined by the faculty who attended. It proved then ineffectual. It was at too late a period. Some fymptoms of the Hydrophobia had already appeared for the two preceding days. This was between the fifth and fixth week from the accident, the moft general period at which hydrophobic fymptoms begin.

As this cafe has never appeared in public, as far as I know, I fhall lay it before my readers, having been obligingly fupplied with it by an ingenious gentleman* who
attended

---

* Mr. R. RHODE, Surgeon to the Firft, or King's regiment of Dragoon Guards, to whofe friendfhip I am indebted for this cafe, affures me, he attended punctually from the time fhe came in till fhe died. He remarks, that fhe gave pertinent anfwers till within a few hours of her death, when delirium ran high, to all fuch queftions as fhe was afked.—Vid. Appendix.

attended lectures at the time, and extracted it from the hofpital books as noted down by the late learned Dr. Drummond, then one of the Clerks, and who was afterwards chofen Profeffor. Having mentioned his name, the medical reader will give full credit to the fidelity and accuracy of the relation.

THE fame means, then, ought to be ufed in cafes of poifon from rabid animals, as we have fhewn would be effectual in preventing the fmall-pox. Let the part bit be deftroyed: let all be cut away. And from the moft rational grounds, and our knowledge of the *modus operandi* of the abforbing fyftem, we may be well fatisfied of the improbability of the Hydrophobia afterwards appearing.

To accomplifh this, various means may be put in practice, as the furgeon may think fit, or the part where the bite is inflicted may feem to require. But, in what ever way

way it is done, I have little hefitation in
afferting, it is the only fure means, yet
known, to obviate death.

SOME authors have recommended ·fuck-
ing the wounded part with the mouth, and
affirm, no ill can follow from the poifon
to the perfon who fucks, as it muft be
ejected with the faliva with which the internal parts of the mouth are conftantly
bedewed, and which, as a farther fecurity,
may be wafhed out afterwards with water.*

D   Exam-

---

* Dr. Berkenhaut is of this opinion : and the fame
has been entertained by the chief of the Latin phyficians, fpeaking of the poifon of·ferpents, &c. I mean
Celfus.—Vid. l. 5. c. 27. "Homo," fays he, "adhi-
" bendus eft, qui vulnus exfugat." And he adds, that
experience confirms the practice. Then gives his opinion: " Nam venenum ferpentis, ut quædam etiam
" venatoria venena, quibus Galli præcipue utuntur,
" non guftu, fed in vulnere nocent." But, at the
fame time, he cautions them to beware left any ulcer
be in the mouth. " Illud interea ante debebit atten-
" dere, ne quod in gingivis, palatove, aliave parte oris
" ulcus habeat." It might almoft be affirmed from
this, that he underftood the laws of abforption, were
we

Examples are adduced to prove this fucceeded in the bite of other poifonous animals, fuch as the viper.

Dr. Berkenhaut feems poffitive the
virus may be fucked without danger. Speaking on the fubject, and of the bite happening in a part of the body where the perfon
cannot reach it with his own mouth, he fays,
" Poffibly he may prevail on fome friend to
" do him this kind office; efpecially when
" I affure him, pofitively affure him, that it
" may be done without the leaft danger.—
" My fon," adds he, " then about eight
" years old, in returning from fchool, was
" bit by a dog in the thigh. My eldeft
" daughter being informed of the accident,
" without the leaft hefitation immediately
" fucked

---

we not certain that it is a much later difcovery. Some
may difpute this; and attribute it to the antients,
when they call to mind Galen's expreffions, viz. " Si
" fitiens balneum ineat, illi fitis fedabitur." Yet I
ftill think the moderns deferve the honour of having
pointed out the proper ufes of the lymphatic fyftem: and
here Doctors Munro and Hunter feem to ftand firft.

" fucked the wound. She had heard me
" fay it might be done with fafety.—The
" dog," the Doctor adds, " was certainly
" not mad; but I relate the ftory in juftice
" to her affectionate intrepidity, which, in
" a young girl, was fomewhat extraordi-
" nary." I perfectly agree with him in
this; and give due praife to the lady for her
affection to her brother.

BUT, neverthelefs, fome doubts may remain on this fubject. Some of the venom
may ftick about the tongue, or fauces, or
about the gums, &c. and be afterwards
fwallowed; nor is it yet clear how far
the poifon may be innocent in the ftomach;
or it may be abforbed from thefe parts. And
fhould any ulcer be in the mouth at the
time, the certainty is therefore greater.
Since the poffibility of this cannot be de-
nied, I am of opinion, that no unneceffary
rifque fhould be run, but all doubt prevented, as our purpofe can be even more
certainly anfwered in another way.

BE-

BESIDES, the analogy of the viper may not, in this cafe, be altogether in point. The *modus operandi* of the poifon of a rabid animal, and the manner the poifon of the viper, and fome other fubftances arreft the organs of life, do not feem to be the fame. We are certain the one acts in confequence of abforption, as already explained : we are not fo certain that either the poifon of the viper, the rattle fnake, or fome other noxious animals, who kill by their fting, or their bite, act in this way. Abforption does not appear to be performed fo quickly, as to produce the effects of the poifon conveyed to the fyftem. The bite of the rattle fnake, we are told, proves fatal, in fome inftances, in a minute—that of a viper in a very few hours.

SOME pigeons which Dr. Areſkine ex-pofed to a female viper were dead in fo fhort a time after the bite as half an hour ; others in about two hours. It would appear from this,

this, that thefe poifons feize on the living principle at once, and deprive it of its powers of action.

In this way opium acts, though we allow it alfo acts by abforption. According to the experiments of Profeffor Munro, it affects thofe nerves to which it is primarily applied, and brings the reft of the nervous fyftem to fympathize, independent of its abforption, and mixture with the blood.*

In this way, likewife, the diftilled water of the Laureo-Cerafus acts. Dr. Nicolls found it kill a dog in lefs than half a minute; much fooner than any abforption could convey it to the fyftem at large. Dr. Madden, likewife, found it prove fatal in a very few hours; and this was the cafe whether it was thrown into the ftomach, or up the rectum in form of clyfter.† As
                                          its

* Eff. & Obf. Crit. & Liter. Vol. III. p. 338.

† Wilmer's Obfervations on poifonous Vegetables.

its effects appear so speedily either after being swallowed, or injected *per anum*, its powers must be exerted on the nervous system immediately, without the intervention of a set of vessels to carry it to the general mass of fluids.

WITH respect to what may follow from incautiously taking the poison of a rabid animal into the mouth, I may mention a case which was lately related to me on very good authority. A young woman had her apron tore and slavered by a mad dog leaping on her and attempting to bite. Fortunately she received no other injury whatever from him, by the timely assistance offered, and the loose part of her cloathing he caught hold of. But imprudently, and without proper reflection, she began to mend the rent in her apron before the part was either sufficiently washed, or well dried; and as imprudently, to save some trouble, we shall suppose, or through habit, instead of cutting off the thread with scissars,

when

when finifhed, fhe bit it off with her teeth.
Lo, what followed! In a few weeks fhe
was feized with Hydrophobia, and died in
the ufual manner of it!

SIMILAR cafes have been obferved by
authors. The following, from Cælius Aurelianus, is almoft a copy, as it would feem,
of what we have now related.—" A cer-
" tain fempftrefs having undertaken to
" mend a cloak tore by the teeth of fome
" mad animal, wetted the feams with her
" tongue, and laid the edges of the rent
" even with her mouth, as fhe fewed,
" in order that the needle might pafs with
" more eafe. In the fpace of three days
" afterwards fhe fell into canine madnefs,
" and died."*

THE

* " Sartrix quædam, quum chlamydem fciffam ra-
" bidis morfibus farciendam fumeret, atque ore ftamina
" componeret, & lingua pannorum futuras lamberet
" affuendo, quo tranfitum acus faceret faciliorum,
" tertia die in rabiem veniffe memoratur."—Vid. Cœl.
Aurel. de morb. acut. l. 3. c. 9. p. 219.

The following, which Hildanus affords, appears ftill a nearer copy.—" A mad dog" he fays, " tore its miftrefs's gown with " its teeth, but wounded no perfon. The " woman, ignorant that the dog was mad, " mended her garment, and bit off the " threads with her teeth. Three months " after fhe died of Hydrophobia." *

We are told by Palmerius of a peafant, who having the canine madnefs, and knowing he foon muft die, defired leave of thofe about him, who had confined him with chains, to kifs his children. He kiffed them, and died foon after. All the children, we are affured, died in the fpace of feven days after of the fame difeafe. †

We have alfo another fimilar example given us by Schenckius. This author tells

us

---

* Hildan. Obf. Chirurg. Cent. 1. No. 86. p. 62.

† Vid. De Morb. Contagios. p. 266.

us of a Mr. Patric, who kiffed his mad dog before he fent it to be ftifled, and perifhed afterwards from Hydrophobia. All this is analogous to what we know of other feeds of difeafes communicated to the habit by the abforbent fyftem. The epithelion on the lips, infide of the mouth, fauces, and tongue, is extremely thin ; the poifon can be moft readily, and even fpeedily taken up by the lymphatics of thefe parts.

But Areteus, and Boerhaave following him, go farther, and affirm, that it may even be communicated by the breath of the mad animal. Aurelian is of the fame opinion, and quotes us an example of it. Here, however, fome room for doubt may remain. The perfon muft be almoft in contact with the animal, as it would feem to me, before he can be in much danger this way. Yet I hope none of my readers, for the fake of their own fafety, in placing themfelves fo near its reach, will ever make the experiment to afcertain the fact.

E

It

It is affirmed, alfo, that an inftrument which has been ufed for killing a mad dog, if left unwiped, will retain for many years enough of the virus to communicate the difeafe. There feems much reafon in this obfervation. We have here, alfo, the analogy of the fmall-pox to fupport it. We know that an infected lancet has given the difeafe long after it had been touched with the variolous matter.

But we are not allowed to reft barely on analogy. An example of this is alfo afforded us. Schenckius relates the cafe of a young man who unfortunately cut his finger in wiping a rufty fword which had been, fome years before, employed to kill a mad dog, and died hydrophobic.

In the bites from ferpents, where the antients have recommended fucking the wound, we find that experience teaches thofe where fuch bites are frequent, not to

truft

truſt the poiſon in their mouths without firſt moiſtening them, as a ſafeguard, with oil.

MR. GOODYEAR, in his account of a Mr. Burdet, an Engliſh merchant, at Aleppo, who was bit by a ſerpent, and who died five hours after, tells us, " that " the people of the country ſay, that if, " as ſoon as one is bit by a ſerpent, they " ſhall ſuck immediately the wound, they " may be ſaved. But they muſt rub firſt " their gums and teeth with oil, that none " of the poiſon may touch any place where " the ſkin is broke, and ſpit out immedi- " ately what they ſuck; every time waſhing " the mouth, and taking more oil."*

ARE not theſe examples, then, beſides what has been advanced, ſufficient, from the nature of the thing itſelf, to leave doubts on our minds relative to the inno-

cence

---

* Vid. Philoſ. Tranſactions Abridg. by Lowthorp. Vol. II. p. 814.

cence and impunity of taking the poifon into the mouth by fucking the wound? and may not a cupping-glafs or a narrow-mouthed phial, where the cupping-glafs cannot be had, anfwer as a fubftitute?* Here no fufpicion of danger can remain. Dr. Berkenhaut himfelf very properly advifes fomething fimilar: "If no furgeon "be prefent," he fays, "take a pretty large "piece of paper; twift it gently, fo that "it may eafily be thruft into a narrow-"mouthed jug; light the paper well, and "having put it into the veffel, fix it tight "over the wound, and let it remain in "that pofition till it may be eafily taken "off. Repeat this operation three or four "times."✝

I SHALL

---

* We are told of a man in London who was bit by a rattle fnake brought from Virginia, and that by fucking the wound he recovered. The Indians, it is faid, cure it the fame way. We have fhewn, however, how cautious the people in the Eaft are; their ufing oil is a prefumptive proof that the omiffion was attended with danger.

✝ P. 77.

I SHALL, without hesitation, then, recommend, and would enforce it, were I
able, a piece to be cut out round the part
wounded, making the incision at the same
time pretty deep, to prevent any accident
from leaving any of the animal's saliva behind. I can see little cruelty here, when
we compare short temporary pain to the
dire scene that we have reason to expect.

THE antients recommend a similar treatment, which Boerhaave, and other authors,
in a great measure, copying from them,
adopt. Prestwick, no doubt, following
them, advises as we have already done.
" The wound should immediately," says
he, " be enlarged, or entirely cut out; then
" apply a cupping-glass, with scarifica-
" tions; after which cauterize the wound,
" washing it daily with salt water and vi-
" negar, or salt dissolved, and keep it open
" with escharotics." *

Dr.

* Prestwick on Poisons, &c.

DR. MEAD readily assents to this method; telling us, " The cure of this poison " is either immediately upon the wound " made, or some days after, before the fear " of water is discovered"—then quotes the antients in support of his opinion—" As in " other venomous bites, so in this, Galen " very wisely advises" proceeds he, " to " enlarge the wound, by making a round " incision about it, to cauterize it with a " hot iron, and apply drawing medicines, " so as to keep it a running *ulcer* at least " forty days. Scarifying and cupping may " answer where this severity is not al-" lowed."*

DR. CULLEN, whose judgement is not, as will be readily allowed, inferior to the most celebrated authors who have treated on the subject, coincides with me in this opinion. " I am, in the first place," says he, " firmly persuaded, that the most " certain

---

* Mead on Poisons, &c.

" certain means of preventing the confe-
" quences of the bite, is to cut out, or
" otherwife deftroy, the part in which the
" bite has been made.. In this," he goes
on, " every body agrees; but with this
" difference, that fome are of opinion that
" it can only be effectual when it is done
" very foon after the wound has been made,
" and they therefore neglect it when this
" opportunity is miffed.   There have been,
" however, no experiments made proper to
" determine this matter; and there are
" many confiderations which lead me to
" think, that the poifon is not immediately
" communicated to the fyftem ; and, there-
" fore, that this meafure of deftroying the
" part may be practifed,. with advantage,
" even many days* after the bite has been
" given."†

SEVERAL

---

* In p. 14 of this Effay a fimilar opinion was hazarded.

† Vid. firft lines Vol. IV. p. 109.

SEVERAL authors mention the actual cautery, *i. e.* burning the part with a red hot iron. This muft likewife, I fhould think, be effectual, if enough be deftroyed. Yet excifion would appear preferable, if we confider the time that muft pafs in the operation of the iron, and, confequently, the augmentation to the fum of pain, which muft be in proportion.

THE part being thus deftroyed, in either of thefe ways it may be judged proper, and the patient fubmits to, the wound muft be kept from healing, either by iffues, blif-tering ointment, or other efcharotics, for feveral months; at leaft fix; but ftill the more certain if longer.

I HAVE feen three cafes where this me-thod was followed. Thefe perfons were all bit by the fame dog (he was certainly mad) in about ten minutes from each other; and in lefs than a quarter of an hour the operation

tion was performed in the hofpital where I then attended. No Hydrophobia ever appeared.

THREE other cafes, as fhall be related hereafter, were treated in a fimilar manner by gentlemen of the faculty in this county.* The dogs that bit the perfons were alfo moft evividently mad, as appeared from their effects.†
I do not go fo far as to declare that they abfolutely owed their lives and prefervation to the judicious treatment that was purfued, becaufe it is impoffible to affert whether the poifon would have ever become active in them; but, allowing the certainty of this, they furely deferve credit, and the patients acknowledgments, as, in thefe cafes, where fo much is at ftake, we fhould act as if we were fure of the poifon taking effect.

DR. FOTHERGILL tells us of two perfons, the mafter and the maid fervant, who

F   were

---

* SUFFOLK.
† Vid. Appendix No. 2 and 3.

were bit by a mad cat. In the maid, the
wound would not heal up, though endeavours were ufed for that purpofe, till after
a confiderable time. The little fcratch
which the mafter received, foon healed.
He became affected with Hydrophobia, and
died : the fervant efcaped. Hence, in his
cafe, abforption took place, and the poifon
was conveyed to the general mafs; in the
other, the running of the fore prevented
this.

It is probable that dry cupping, and afterwards fcarifying the part, might fucceed in the prevention of abforption; but it
is beft to be on the fafe fide, and extirpate
at once, where the part will admit of it.

The fame may be faid of a cauftic;
though I think it more certain than cupping, provided it be long enough applied,
and an efchar, fufficiently large and deep,
formed; the part, in like manner as in extirpation, to be kept from healing.

Some-

SOMETIMES it happens that the part wounded is unfavourable for extirpation; nay, for being even long kept open. This will be found the cafe when either the lips, or parts about the face are bit. In any of thefe, long running fores prove very trouble-fome; and are fuch as few people will fub-mit to. Extirpation of part of either the upper or under lip, has likewife many other inconveniencies: a fcar muft remain alto-gether unfeemly, rendering the countenance extremely difagreeable.

THIS, unluckily, happened to be the part where the bite was inflicted in a late cafe, alluded to in the beginning of this effay. Cauftics, however, were applied, and other proper means ufed, foon after it was received, by a gentleman learned and eminent in the medical world, then called to the patient's affiftance. That they did not fucceed, might in part arife from the cauftic not being applied to every part of the wound;

wound; but with as much, nay more, probability, from fome of the dog's faliva getting into the mouth, and adhering about the gums or infide of the lip, from whence it was afterwards abforbed; for " the lip " was torn a good deal. The teeth" (of the dog) " had gone through and through, and had tore out a piece."*

IN fuch cafes the phyfician has a moft difficult part to act. If he pays too great an attention to appearances, he may fall into the oppofite extreme, and lofe his patient from lenity and regard to his looks. If he boldly advifes extirpation, and his patient furvives, he may not efcape blamelefs, but incur his difpleafure as long as he lives for disfiguring him, as he will call it.

THE moft unfavourable places are thofe about the face; and of thefe, the cheeks, nofe, and lips, are moft fo. The fore part of

---

* Mr. Hunter's letter to the author.

of neck, alfo, is not without inconveniencies. Yet it is better to act on fuch
occafions, than to run the hazard of fuffer-
ing the patient's life to fall a facrifice without attempting fo rational a prophylactic.
Should the worft take place, we have difcharged our duty, without leaving our patient to chance for an efcape.

WHERE the wound has been made in
the cheek, and has penetrated through, by
which fome of the poifonous faliva muft
touch the infide, and thus efcape the knife,
the cauftic, or other fuch means as is ufed,
we fhould direct the patient, provided we
fee him foon after, to wafh and fcour the
infide of the mouth with detergents; falt
and water, a weak folution of the vegetable
alkili, and fuch like. And this fhould be
often repeated, ufing a piece of fponge to
abforb all the moifture, and carefully wafh-
ing it every time it is ufed, while the knife
or the cauftic is externally employed to
deftroy the adjacent lymphatics.

CUP-

CUPPING may likewife be ufed here, but I can conceive little advantage that is to be obtained by fcarifications; yet, fhould the furgeon, or medical man called in, think them material, I have no objection to the practice

IF we confide in thefe means which reafon approves, fhould they not fucceed, we know the obftacles, and can pronounce them be-yond the power of human fkill : for if an active particle gets a little forward into the mouth of a lymphatic, what human fkill can tell the part where it lies ? and where is the fpecific that will overtake, and arreft it in its flight ?

AMONG other directions which **Dr. Fo-**thergill gives, is that of enlarging the wound by gunpowder; this is to be moift-ened and a little put on the part, and then fet on fire. This he confiders as a good way of difcharging the poifon fuddenly:

we

we fuppofe this is brought to pafs by the fhock given to the part, while at the fame time it forms fuch a kind of wound as is not readily difpofed to heal. In fuch circumftances as we have already mentioned, where the wound cannot be enlarged with fafety, he recommends a blifter, and this to be kept open as long as conveniently may be done.

LET no faith whatever be put in thofe medicines called fpecifics, and certain preventatives. It will be trufting moft certainly to a broken reed. Experience has fhewn them not only fallible, but really trifling; and as we now know the compofition, it is no difficult matter to prove that fuch ingredients as compofe them are, fingly or united, altogether inadequate fuccefsfully to oppofe the evil.

WE fhall pafs over that of Aefchrion, compofed of burned crabs, as mentioned by Galen and Oribafius; the famous opi-

ates

ates of Scribonius Largus; the boasted powder of Palmerius; that of Turpeth mineral, so much extolled by Dr. James; the tin and mithridate, on which Myern and Grew bestow so much praise; also the root of the dog-briar, or rose,* said to be discovered in holy visions; the liver of the mad dog, broiled and eaten; the pimpinella, (Burnet) of Henry II. King of France, which he is said to have discovered on his death bed to his physician Fernelius; with several others; and only take notice of two or three now in common use, and high estimation with the public; and some of them extolled, even at this day, by physi- of abilities and learning.

One that seems to claim our special attention is the Ormskirk medicine. Since its reputation has stood so high for many years,

---

* Spongia Cynnorhodia : P. Boccone wrote a treatise on its virtues. The Scicilians call it Sanatodos; All Heal.—It is called by us Dog-rose, because celebrated in the cure of *rabies canina*. The part used is an excrescence growing about its root.

years, and ftill is looked on as infallible by many, efpecially in the northern diftricts of England.

DR. FOTHERGILL is amongft thofe who began to doubt its virtues. The melancholy cafe of Mr. Belamy, which he attended, and for which it had been bought of the perfon authorifed to fell it, and ufed ftrictly according to the directions, gave grounds for doubts, which its fallibility fince has ferved to confirm.

LET us now enquire what this celebrated noftrum is. According to the analyfis it underwent fome years ago, we fhall find, it is not compofed of a fingle active ingredient.

IN the year 1777, Dr. Heyfham, then a candidate for a degree, who wrote his inaugural differtation on *rabies canina*, inftituted five experiments, in order to find out its component parts. Thefe were made with

G   the

the addition of water, the nitrous and vi-
trolic acids. They were repeated by Dr.
Black, Profeſſor of Chymeſtry, with the
ſame reſult; and, conſequently, there can
remain little room for ſuſpicion of their
accuracy. From theſe it appeared, that
the baſis of the medicine was chalk; and,
relying on its powers, a theory was hazarded,
relative to the nature of the poiſon of the
rabid animal, which it is not our buſineſs
here to examine.

In a word, from the analyſis of this
eminent Profeſſor, and his ingenious pupil,
the whole compoſition appears to be as
follows, viz. Half an ounce of powdered
chalk; ten grains of allum; three drams
of Armenian bole; one dram of the powder
of elecampane root; and ſix drops of oil of
aniſe. Such is the medicine on which the
public have placed ſuch high hopes, and
implicit confidence!

I NEED

I NEED not tell my medical readers, if any of them fhould think thefe pages worth a perufal, that chalk is a mere abforbent; that allum is an aftringent; that Armenian bole, likewife poffeffes a degree, though a fmall one, of aftringency; and that the root of elecampane is confidered as fuch an in-active, infignificant fubftance, that our re-formed pharmacopoeias have long ago re-jected it from the number of the articles of the *materia medica*; and as to the addition of a few drops of oil of anife, they can be of no other ufe than to warm the medicine a little, and give it a more grateful flavor.

NEXT, in order of celebrity, comes the Tonquin medicine, a noftrum not lefs noted fome time ago, and even now exhibited, than this one. What, then, fhall we fay, of it ?—very little more than of the former. We owe it to the well-meant, though mif-taken endeavours, of Sir George Cobb, who, near forty years ago, brought it from Tonquin, whence it derives its name, as of inefti-

ineftimable value, and as conftantly infallible among the Chinefe; but experience,
in many inftances, fhews the contrary with
us, and proves its inefficacy.

LET us now examine its compofition;
and we fhall find it to be only twenty-four
grains of native, and as many of factitious
cinnabar; with fixteen grains of mufk,
powdered, and mixed together. Few comments farther, we apprehend, are neceffary
on the fubject. The bare mention of the
articles feems enough. We may, however,
take notice of what feveral eminent chy-
mifts have done before us, that native and
factitious cinnabar are one and the fame
thing; and we may alfo add, with fome of
thefe, that all the cinnabars are inert, and
poffefs no active powers whatever.

NATIVE cinnabar is the ore of mercury,
being a compound of fulphur with this me-
tallic fubftance. And is there a perfon of
the leaft chymical knowledge, or experience
in

in its exhibition, and obfervation of its effects, that does not know this, and that fulphur has the pecular property of rendering mercury inert?

THE other ingredient, viz. mufk, is an antifpafmodic. So far it may feem ufeful in a difeafe, fuch as Hydrophobia, where fo violent fpafms take place in the throat; but it has not fufficient power to oppofe and remove the malady. Yet, we muft own, that it appears a better medicine than the Ormfkirk, fince it has at leaft a fmall part of one active ingredient in it.

WITH refpect to Dr. Mead's famous powder, I fhall only mention that it was a compofition of afh-coloured ground liverwort *(lichen cinereus terreftris)* and black pepper; the former, the ingredient which he depended on, and to which the virtues of the powder were attributed. Materia medica writers tell us, this lichen is a warm diuretic; but, from the tafte, little or no

warmth

warmth can be difcovered in it; and it is a general rule, which, we believe, will be found to hold good in the vegetable kingdom, that where little or no fenfible qualities are difcoverable, little or no virtues for the removal of difeafes fhall be found to exift.*

In the Tranfactions of the Royal Society, No. 237, we find a Mr. Dampier communicating to the members, fome remarkable effects that had been attributed to a vegetable fubftance, which was called Jew's-ear,† in the difeafe we are now confidering. In the year 1721, a powder, compofed and named as above, was inferted into the London Phamacopoeia, at the defire of an eminent phyfician, who put great confidence in its virtues. ‡

In

---

* Infipidæ & inodoræ vim medicam vix exercent. Lin.

† Tremella Auricula of Linnæus.

‡ Dr. Mead, on Sir Hans Sloane's authority, changed the Tremella for the Lichen Cinereus Terreftris, fuppofing that Mr. Dampier muft have been miftaken, and ufed the former for the latter.—Vid. Berkenhaut.

IN 1745 a new edition of a treatife relative to the mechanical account of poifons
was laid before the public. Here the fame
medicine and method of cure is recommended, viz. V. Section, and the cold bath,
which was to be ufed every morning fafting for one month, in addition to the powder; and on the pompous authority of its
fuccefs in thirty years practice: but an addition of nearly forty years more proves, beyond a doubt, its infignificancy. It is only
to be obferved farther, that this did not
efcape the penetration of Boerhaave, who
ranks this among thofe infignificant trifles
that muft deceive whoever place their truft
in them.* To collect, and relate the cafes
wherein this has failed, is needlefs: they
are many; and the public have at length
configned it to merited neglect.

IF we examine the accounts of hydrophobic cafes, we fhall likewife find feveral,

where

* Lewis's New Difpenf.

where the Ormſkirk has been attended with no better ſucceſs : enough, in my opinion, to induce us to hold it in a very different light, from what many continue to view it in. Had we only that of Mr. Bellamy, it ſhould leſſen our faith, as one poſitive proof of its failure, is worth an hundred negative proofs of its ſucceſs, ſince it becomes impoſſible to tell, whether the perſon bit, and who takes it, would have been affected with the diſeaſe, conſequently, whether it had any ſhare as a prophylactic. But we have three others by Dr. Vaughan; and I am ſorry to add, that a recent inſtance of its failure in this county* makes another.

In this laſt caſe, both it and the Tonquin, as alſo mercury, were adminiſtered, with ſtrict attention, from a few hours after the accident till ſymptoms of Hydrophobia made their appearance, which was not till ſix weeks after.

" ALL

SUFFOLK.

"ALL the means recommended were "ufed in Mafter R-----'s cafe. I faw him "a few hours only after the bite.—He "took the Ormfkirk medicine by the di-"rection of Mr. Barry, who fells it, there-"fore we muft fuppofe it was properly "given. He alfo took the Tonquin me-"dicine, viz. mufk, cinnabar, &c. as alfo "rubbed in mercurial ointment till his "mouth was fore."—My refpectable and learned correfpondent adds, " My whole "dependence was on the *cauftic*, but did "not object to the others being given."*

THIS cafe proves more, indeed, than we intended. It proves that mercury is like-wife ufelefs as a preventative, fince it had here fo fair a trial, and yet Hydrophobia took place.

BUT my opponents will fay, perhaps, it proves more than we wifhed; fince it

H   fhews

* Mr. John Hunter.

shews that the use of the cauftic, one of thofe very means we have ventured to recommend, was, in like manner, ineffectual. This, however, I refufe to admit; becaufe, the part was unfavourable : for it was the lip— and this alfo, cut quite through, where fome of the dog's faliva muft have fallen on the gums, or been fcattered to fome diftance over the infide of the mouth, or cheeks, or both. " The lip was tore a good deal. " The teeth had gone through and through, " and had tore out a piece."*

THOUGH the part had all been deftroyed, fince fome of the particles of the infected faliva muft have been thrown beyond the part bitten, and, of courfe, beyond the reach of either knife, or cauftic, &c. it was not in the power of man to fay where to find it.

THIS being fo, as is a rational induc-tion, it proves no more than what has been
already

---

* Mr. Hunter's letter to the author.

already admitted, and even pointed out, that there are some parts of the body, more than others, unfavourable either for excision, cauftic, or cautery; and that thefe are about the face; and chiefly the lips and cheeks. Hence the objection muft fall to the ground, and can militate nothing againft our general doctrine, with refpect to other parts of the body not liable to fuch inconveniences. The legs, the arms, the thighs, the trunk of the body, and even the fore part of the neck, or the face, will admit of excision, &c. as will alfo the nofe, though the danger in this laft is fomewhat greater. The cheeks and lips, then, are the chief places where excifion may be doubful; and the reafons we have given above.

YET thefe are by no means fuch as fhould difcourage us. Let us apply the preventative means in our power, I mean the rational means already pointed out; and let us be careful to touch every furface where the dog's teeth have gone, if we ufe ·

the

the cauftic, and let feveral floughs be thrown off. Let us wafh out the mouth with falt and water, or a folution of the vegetable alkali, and then with oil, as already recommended, and we have reafon to hope for the beft.

NEXT comes the cold bath. From al-moft the earlieft ages of medicine, this has been practifed as a cure; and in later times as a preventative of Hydrophobia. The limits we have prefcribed to ourfelves will not allow of a minute difcuffion of this point; but fince, at this day, it is celebrated, by many learned phyficians, as a certain pro-phylactic; and fince cafes are adduced in fupport of its efficacy, I find myfelf under the neceffity of touching a little on the fub-ject. All I can do, it is true, is to give my own opinion; this is incumbent on me; and, in a word, is, that after an im-partial confideration of all circumftances, for and againft the practice, I am free to confefs a difbelief of its virtues.

IN

In the firſt place, I can find no rational grounds to reſt on. The effects of ſea-bathing, which reaſon bids me expect, are by no means adequate to the deſtroying, or rendering the poiſon inert. I ſee but two ways in which it can act, viz. Firſt, as a purgative; and yet it muſt be here a very gentle one. In the manner of ſuddenly throwing the patient into the ſea, &c. a ſmall quantity of the water may be ſwallowed—but diſſections of drowned people ſhew, that very little deſcends into the ſtomach in this act. Death here takes place from ſuffocation. But we ſhall allow a little to get beyond the cardia, enter the ſtomach, and then the alimentary canal, from the obſervation above, the caſe is nothing altered. Secondly, it acts as a general coroborant of the ſyſtem.

But all this is little to the purpoſe. Though we purge, we cannot purge away the poiſon, which is far removed from our

reach

reach here; and though we ftrengthen the fibres of the body, we cannot ftop the pro-cefs of abforption. Nay, the powers of the lymphatic fyftem would feem thence to be encreafed, and the poifon the more readily, and effectually, carried to the ge-neral mafs.

I AM happy to find eminent men adopt my fide of the queftion. Dr. Fothergill, Dr. Flack, and Dr. Berkenhaut, all concur with me in it.—The laft, in a judicious review he has taken of this, and feveral of our noted prophylactics and fpecifics, is particularly pointed on this part of his fubject.*

IN the Philofophical Tranfactions, No. 445, a cafe is related by Mr. Nourfe, of a lad bit in the thumb by a mad dog. He was ten times dipped in the fea, and took alfo, we are told, the famous fpecific

of

---

* Vid. Eff. on the Bite of a Mad Dog. p. 56 & feq.

of that day, the pulvis antyliſſus, for no leſs
than forty days.—Was he cured thereby?
No; for it is added, he died hydrophobic
nineteen months after: in the interim,
however, he was cut for the ſtone, and
perfectly recovered from the operation.＊

CELSUS, I know, recommends it ſtrong-
ly; not, however, as a prophylactic, but as a
remedy for the removal of the Hydrophobia
itſelf.   He obſerved the patient's inability
to ſwallow liquids, and ſaw, at the ſame
time, his great deſire for them: in order,
then, that his thirſt might be quenched, he
directs the ſufferer to be thrown headlong,
and unexpectedly, into a fiſh-pond, and
there ducked ſeveral times, that " his thirſt,
" and

＊ In the Philoſophical Tranſactions, No. 191, Sir
Tho. Myern, deſcribing different compoſitions, which
he calls Cures for the Bite of a Mad Dog, mentions
ſea-bathing. " Let the party," ſays he, " be nine
" times plunged in the ſea, while he is faſting, as ſoon
" as may be after the bite."—I need ſcarcely take
notice of the ſuperſtitious regard paid to the number
nine.

" and dread of water, might be cured at
" one and the fame time."*

It is needlefs to make any comments on
this treatment. The reader will eafily per-
ceive it was founded on a miftake. Though
fome of the water might get into the ftomach, yet the inability of fwallowing could
not be removed, nor the *aquæ horror* become lefs thereby. From this, however,
the practice feems to have flid down to pof-
terity, and the original intention, miftaken

as

---

* —" Miferrimum (Hydrophobia) genus morbi:
" in quo fimul æger & fiti, & aquæ metu cruciatur.
" Quo oppreffis in angufto fpes eft. Sed *unicum tamen*
" *remedium eft*, nec opinantem in pifcinam non ante ei
" provifam projicere, &, fi natandi fcientiam non ha-
" bet, modo merfum bibere pati, modo attollere; fi
" habet, interdum deprimere, ut invitus quoque aqua
" fatietur. Sic enim, & fitis, et aquæ metus tollitur."
—After this half-drowning, to guard againft the debilitating effects of fuch rough treatment, the patient is
directed to be thrown into warm oil, immediately on
coming out of the fifh-pond.—" A pifcina protinus in
" oleum calidum demittendus eft."—Celf. de Medicin.
l. 5. c. 27.

as it was, exchanged for one on no furer a foundation, viz. that of a prophylactic.

WE find, that in the days of Van Helmont, who lived fo late as the fixteenth century, it was only ufed in the Hydrophobia. This author relates, that he faw a patient ducked in this manner in the Netherlands, near Ghent, at a place on the fea coaft, called *Sluce*. Weights were tied, we are told, to his feet, fo that he could be kept under water, or hauled up by the rope faftened under his arms, at any time they pleafed.

HE was thrice ducked. The firft time they let him down, he was fuffered to remain under water *ad fpatium miferere,* which is about a minute and half; a fufficient time, I think, to fuffocate him, though not irrecoverably. At the fecond and third times, he was allowed only to remain *ad fpatium falutationis Angelicæ, i. e.*

I   about

about ten feconds.* This man was a cooper from Ghent. It is added, he was cured by this treatment.

The cafe of a girl is related in the Hiftory of the Academy of Sciences at Paris, faid there to be cured in the fame manner; and a gentleman now living, of refpectable medical abilities, thinks he faw a perfon prevented from Hydrophobia by the fame means. Two were bit—one ufed the feabathing a confiderable time, and efcaped; the other did not bathe, and died. But there is the greateft reafon to conclude, from reflecting on the matter, that had the fea-bath never been ufed in this cafe, the perfon would have efcaped, becaufe he was not really infected; and, had the other bathed with all the diligence recommended,

he

Vid. Berkenhaut on the Bite of a mad dog. Pfalm 51 begins with the word *Miferere*: Dr. B. counted his ftop watch while a friend read over this prayer—he found the time one minute and thirty-five feconds; and the Salutatio Angelica only ten feconds.

he would have died, becaufe he was really infected.

MORGAGNI mentions two cafes where the patients died, though the cold bath had been ufed. In the one, the patient died the night following; and in the other cafe, a little after being taken out. On the whole, to ufe the words of Dr. Berkenhaut, " the " inftances in which it has failed, as a pro- " phylactic remedy, are innumerable."

SEVERAL, even of the antients, put but little faith in it, no doubt, from the little fuccefs they faw attending the practice. Cæl. Aurelianus reprobates it, as injurious; Salius and others, from their experience, declared againft its utility; and, from what Morgagni faw, we may eafily conclude what muft be the degree of his faith.

DR. MEAD exprefsly tells us, that he knew many die raving mad, who had undergone this treatment. Default, who has

wrote

wrote on this difeafe, tells us, he has feen feveral proofs of its inefficacy in one year. Four men were bit by a mad wolf; two of them were dipped, yet died within the fpace of one year. Choifel, who has alfo wrote on the fubject, gives his teftimony againft it, faying, " not one of thofe who depended " folely on this remedy furvived the bite " more than thirty-three days."—It is need-lefs to quote examples; we find but too many on record of its failure.

I SHALL reft, then, with the mention only of one more; I mean the gentleman whofe cafe is related to us by Dr. Munck-ley in the Medical Tranfactions.—The af-ternoon of the fame day on which he was bit, he fet off for the fea fide; this was the 11th of July, 1760.—He ftayed there ten days, during which he bathed conftantly; yet, in the fpace of about fix weeks after, he became hydrophobic, and died. The words of an eminent gentleman, defervedly high in the public efteem, may be quoted on this

occa-

occafion.—" I knew," fays he, " where " there were twenty-one people bit by one " dog. Nothing was done for any of them, " and only one was taken ill. If they had " all taken medicines, then it would have " been faid, that they only loft one out of " twenty-one."—Now, had all thefe people bathed in the fea, it would have had the character of a preventative in no lefs than twenty cafes out of twenty-one; fufficient, furely, as it would feem, to make us rely on its virtues.

Several authors have infifted largely on the ufe of mercury. Among thefe are to be reckoned Dr. James, the Baron Van Sweiten, and Sauvages; and later ftill, Dr. de Laffone, Firft Phyfician to the King of France.* Dr. Cullen, likewife, is inclined to think well of it, and fays, its utility feems to be more fupported by experience,

than

---

* Vid. Methode eprouvée pour le Traitment de la Rage.

than moſt other medicines.* But, I apprehend, we have no right to determine
any thing with certainty in favour of the
practice. On the contrary, it has failed in
ſo many inſtances on record, where it was
not only tried, but its uſe puſhed to a conſiderable length, that we have great reaſon
to ſuſpect its virtues; and, perhaps, might
be juſtified in conſigning it to the ſame ob-
livion with other noted ſpecifics.

WE are told by Dr. de Laſſone, that it
was tried in eleven out of fifteen perſons
who were bit, and tore by a mad wolf on
the 8th and 9th of December, 1775, within
twenty-four hours of each other. Three
of theſe, it ſeems, truſting to powdered oy-
ſter-ſhells, (a remedy, it is to be obſerved,
ſomewhat ſimilar to our Ormſkirk) died in
a few days raving mad. Alſo a fourth, a
young woman, who did not apply for relief till two days before her death, and after
Hydrophobia had commenced.

DR

---

† Vid. Firſt Lines of the Pract. of Phyſic. Vol. IV.

Dr. Blaise, a Phyfician of Cluny, had the care of the remaining eleven. They began a mercurial courfe. One man, after ufing it for ten days, became hydrophobic, and died forty-eight hours after; and, it is added, he died placidly, and in his fenfes. A fecond ufed it near a month, then became affected, was furious, and died in two days comatofe. A third, a boy, who ufed it, as alfo fome antifpafmodic medicines, for eighteen days, was then removed home by his friends, who fuppofed him fafe, but who, three weeks afterwards, died. A fourth was difcharged, likewife, apparently well, after ufing the mercury a confiderable time; but, lo! fix weeks after, he, alfo, became hydrophobic, and died. Here, then, are eight out of the fifteen, loft; four of whom were treated with mercury: the remaining feven have their cure attributed to it; but, is it not as reafonable to fuppofe, they never were infected?

If

IF we draw a comparifon, it will be found, that a much larger proportion than feven out of fifteen, bit by animals really mad, efcape the infection. " Twenty-one " were bit," fays Mr. Hunter, " by a mad " dog; nothing was done for any of them, " yet only one fell ill." This is, furely, a convincing proof of what we now advance. It is added, in Monf. Blaife's account, that all thofe who recovered had ufed the mer- cury above a month.

IN the cafe of Abraham Palmer, who was bit in 1783, as lately laid before the public,* we find mercury had a tolerable fair trial; but it was with equal bad fuc- cefs. I fhall give my readers an abftract of it in the appendix.

DR. HOULSTON† has given us an ex- tract of a letter from a friend of his on the
conti-

---

* Vid. Med. Commen. Vol. I.
† Vid. Lond. Med. Journ, Vol. V. No. 4.

continent, wherein, among other information, an account is given of nine perſons, in the ſame priſon, bit by the ſame dog; yet only one of them became hydrophobic. And, it is added, that he was neither the firſt nor the laſt bit, nor yet the moſt wounded. He fell ſick, it ſeems, more than four months after the bite, was under Dr. Houlſton's correſpondent's care, and died, it is obſerved, convulſed, but without delirium.

The caſe we have ſeveral times had occaſion to allude to, as giving riſe to theſe remarks, and ſtill ſo freſh in our memory, was treated, among other things, with mercury.—" He alſo rubbed in mercurial ointment till his mouth was ſore,"* but with no better ſucceſs than thoſe we have pointed out.

While Dr. de Laſſone and Dr. Blaiſe extol ſo much the uſe of mercury, behold

K   the

---

* Mr. Hunter's letter to the author.

the auxiliary they call in to their aid ! nothing lefs than the very means I have been endeavouring to eftablifh as the moft certain and rational prophylactic. His words (Dr. de Laffone) are, " It is moft certain, that " the remedies we have employed, have been " very fuccefsful;" (is it becaufe feven out of fifteen efcaped ?) " but they would have " been much more fo, had they been ufed " early; and particularly, if, *almoft immedi-* " *ately* after the bite, thofe external means " had been made ufe of, which appear to me " indifpenfably neceffary, viz. deep fcarifi- " cations, cutting away the lacerated parts, " and thofe adjoining to the wounds; the " cautery; applying cupping-glaffes; and " eftablifhing copious fuppuration, for a " long time, in the part bit."—Then he gives his reafons, which are as follows :— " Becaufe, it fometimes happens, that the " faliva is lodged in the cellular membrane, " where it remains, as it were, fixed, and " inert, till, brought into action by fome " caufe, it enters into the circulation, af-
" fects

" fects the nerves, and produces the train
" of fymptoms of this moft terrible of
" difeafes." *

On the whole, we have feveral proofs
pofitive of its failure, though it was dili-
gently and properly applied; and, as already remarked, one of thefe alone, is of
more weight in forming an opinion, than
an hundred proofs prefumptive, fince we
had no certainty whether or not there was
any infection communicated, that would
have ever become active.

It

---

* Among fome remarks by Mr. Odoardi in the
Memoirs of the Paris Royal Soc. of Med. Vol. II. we
are told of nine perfons, bit by a mad wolf, all of
whom were treated by mercurial friction, and efcaped,
except one, who was put under the care of another
furgeon, and was not treated with it. He died hydrophobic on the forty-fixth day after.—Vid. Med. Com.
Vol. VIII. for 1782 and 1783.—Are thefe the fame
we took notice of, as mentioned in the Lond. Med.
Journ. for 1784?—It is not faid in this laft, that any
treatment had been purfued.

IT is needlefs to enquire who was the firft propofer of this remedy. . We may only take notice, that it appears to be of no very modern date. Among others, we find Palmerius directing it to be applied to the wounds inflicted by a rabid animal. But it was in the form, and for the purpofe only of an efcharotic, viz. fublimate, and red precipitate; that the wound might be enlarged, and the difcharge thereby encreafed.

DESAULT afterwards arofe, and advanced a theory, or rather an opinion (for he did not endeavour to prove it) that canine madnefs was owing to minute vermicles. And as mercury was well known to be a powerful anthelmintic, he proceeded, on this fuppofition, to adminifter it.* And, like other gentlemen, who wifh to celebrate, and eftablifh their favourite fpecific, he proceeds to relate cafes of its fuccefs, as he calls them.

He

---

* Vid. Default Sur la Rage. 1734, in 12mo.

He alfo applied it in form of unction to the wounds. To this he joined the ufe of Palmerius's powder, which, for the curiofity of fuch of our readers as do not know it, we have added in the appendix.

Though Van Sweiten is inclined to fpeak favourably of mercury, yet he is ingenuous enough to confefs alfo its failure, and hints at a cafe in the Medical Effays, which we hold as a very convincing proof of it. For we are told there, of a youth bit by a mad dog, who was then troubled with a gonorrhœa, and who took at the fame time his dofe of *mercurius dulcis*, and every following morning his purge; yet the frequent ufe of this medicine did not prevent him from perifhing; for, a month after the wound was inflicted, he died hydrophobic.* Here, as we generally find is the cafe, the wound foon healed up.

Dr.

_____

* Vid. Med. Eff. Edinb. Vol V. part 2. p. 590.

DR. DICKSON likewife tried it, without effect. In the beginning of January, 1767, John Brown, thirteen years of age, was immediately carried, after the bite of a mad dog, to the London hofpital. The parts affected were the right cheek, and fhoulder. Thefe were fcarified, and allowed to bleed freely; then mercurial ointment was rubbed on them, twice a day, for ten days, without, however, producing forenefs of the gums. Having no other complaints, the Doctor adds, he was difmiffed the hofpital at the end of three weeks, and continued well for three months; when he fuddenly felt a pain in the bitten part, and, in a few days after, died hydrophobic.

IT is argued, by feveral who think well of it, that though it has failed when the body was faturated therewith, and this kept up even for a long time, yet it is not fufficient to condemn its ufe; for, if a falivation fhould be raifed, and continued for a fufficient

ficient time, they are of opinion, there is great reafon to hope for fuccefs. Dr. Cheyne is among thofe who wifh to inculcate this notion.—" The cure cannot be " certain," fays he, " unlefs it be brought " to rife to a quick falivation."—His reafoning is as follows :—" For, as the effect " of this poifon is quick, fo muft that be " of its antidotes."*—I fhall offer nothing againft this opinion, but the want of fupport from experience.

OTHERS who favor this remedy, applied in this way, argue, with refpect to its utility, on the grounds of analogy, from the encreafed flow of faliva occafioned by it, and the fame encreafed difcharge from the falival glands, always obfervable in perfons under Hydrophobia. It is fuppofed, that nature makes efforts to throw off the poifon by thefe outlets ; and that if it be affifted by mercury, which is well known to exert

a

---

* Vid. Defeafes of Body and Mind. p. 103.

a peculiar power over thefe, there feems to be ample reafon, it is thought, to hope for fuccefs; yet, experience, as we have endeavoured to point out, by no means confirms the practice.

ANOTHER reafon for giving mercury, is built on the analogy of its fpecific powers over the venereal difeafe, where the poifon, like that of the rabid animal, is drunk up, and carried into the habit by the lymphatics. But it furely does not follow, that becaufe it may be a fpecific over one fort of poifon, it is fo over others entering the body by the fame channels. The fmall-pox is an appofite example. Mercury was never found to kill the variolous poifon, nor prevent the appearance of the difeafe, when once the habit was tainted. This, then, is a weak argument, and totally unfit to give fupport to the caufe for which it is produced. Befides, we found that faturating the body failed; but faturating the body with mercury cures the venereal difeafe, equally well,

nay

nay better, than when falivation is raifed;
therefore, if it was a fpecific for killing the
poifon of a rabid animal, it fhould prove
effectual in this way, as well as in the other.
The arguments drawn from this fource, I
think, are not tenable.

Dr. Berkenhaut, mentioning Default
and the Jefuit Choifel, relative to their fuppofed fuccefs with mercury, and telling us,
that as he finds where it was thought to be
fuccefsful, it was always applied in form of
ungent, that in feveral cafes it was, at the
fame time, internally adminiftered, con-
cludes, that the cures attributed to it, muft
have depended folely on the fat, with which
the mercury was united.—" For, evidence"
he fays, " is wanting to prove, that the
" internal, without the external application
" of the ointment, will prevent the Hy-
" drophobia—May we not, therefore, ha-
" zard a conjecture," he goes on, " that
" the lard, or fat, of which the mercurial
" ointment is made, is the real preferva-
L " tive ?"

" tive ?"—Here the Doctor feems to allow,
that cures have been made by it, which appears to me to want fufficient evidence.—
" Is not this conjecture powerfully fup-
" ported," he continues, " by the analogy
" between the canine poifon, and that of
" the viper, which is effectually deftroyed
" by the viper's fat, or oil of any kind ap-
" plied to the part."—He acknowledges,
however, that this is mentioned merely as
a conjecture, to be determined by future
experiments.

In the firft place, we ventured it as our
opinion, in another part of thefe obfervations, that there is little, if any, analogy
between the poifon of a viper, and thofe
poifons that become deftructive from entering the habit by the lymphatics, on account
of the fuddennefs of death attending the bite
of the viper, which feems to take place, not
by abforption, but by a peculiar power it
exerts over the principle of life.—Secondly,
that the oil does not prevent Hydrophobia,
appears

appears from its failure in a late cafe, already alluded to, not to mention others on record, where the ointment had alfo a trial—for, " he rubbed in mercurial ointment till his " mouth was fore"*—yet his difeafe, as the unhappy event proved, was neither pro-tracted, nor cured by it.

THE ingenious Dr. Houlfton, it is true, reafons very fpecioufly for it : " Is the in-" ference juft," he fays, " that becaufe the " action of mercurials applied, for three, " or four days at moft, will not cure the " difeafe in its laft hafty ftage, the fame " remedy would have been of no avail in " the interval between the bite and the at-" tack ?—During that period, a gradual and " fufficient action of the mercury might " have been excited ; whereas, when the " Hydrophobia has appeared, there is fcarce-" ly ever time for any fuch effect."† The cafes

---

* Mr. Hunter's letter to the author.

† Vid. Med. Comm. Vol. VIII. p. 306:

cafes we have already mentioned would
feem to fet this entirely afide; yet I fhall
ftill be defirous to fee farther experiments,
either to condemn or confirm its ufe;
though, upon the whole, from thefe now
related, without troubling the reader either
with quotations of more, or farther reafoning on the fubject, it would appear, that
mercury is as feeble an aid to truft to, as
others taken notice of.*

I AM

---

* Among others, we muft not omit fome mention,
of Mr. Douglas, a furgeon, who was a great advocate
for mercury, and who wrote fome obfervations on the
fubject.—Dr. James prefents us with a paper of his at
large.—Mr. D. in a poftfcript, takes notice of a differtation he had then in the prefs, wherein he confiders,
it feems, both antient and modern antidotes.—" From
" whence," we are told, " it will evidently appear,
" by fair analogical reafonings, and various experi-
" ments, that, that antidote (mercury) which moft
" effectually expels the malignant and deadly poifon
" conveyed by *the fling of a h-rl-t's tail*, muft alfo
" be the beft antidote againft the fling of the fcorpion,
" the bite of the viper, rattle fnake, and all the fer-
" pents in the Eaft or Weft Indies."—We have refufed
already to admit reafonings drawn from fuch analogy.—
Vid. Dr. James on Canine Madnefs. p. 130.

I AM inclined, alſo, to believe, much miſchief has been done by the injudicious exhibition of this mineral ſubſtance, in every diſeaſe in which it has been uſed. How many ruined conſtitutions do we almoſt daily behold, from the injudicious uſe of it for the cure of complaints proceeding from unclean embraces! Few know its powers over the human body, compared to the numbers who raſhly undertake to preſcribe it. For, this not only depends on the know-ledge of the ſubſtance, in all the combina-tions in which it is uſed, but on an intimate acquaintance with the ſtructure, and uſes of the various parts of the machine (and a complicated one it truly is) together with their pathology, whoſe irregular motions they pretend to rectify,

IT requires nicety to diſtinguiſh, how far we ſhould proceed in its exhibition, even in thoſe complaints, where its uſe is plainly indicated, and where the cure may chiefly

depend

depend on it. All thefe things we call medicines, are extraneous fubftances, *i. e.* foreign to the body; not being ufeful in fupplying nourifhment, or other deficiencies from the wafte it undergoes; or, in other words, they are poifons of various degrees of ftrength, according to their various natures; fome of them highly deleterious, and fpeedily and powerfully active, and lethiferous. According, then, to their powers, and the particular habit they enter, they exert their force, always exciting inordinary commotions. They cannot, therefore, be exhibited with abfolute innocence and impunity. In order, however, to prevent a greater evil, a fmaller muft be fuftained. Here is their utility; and here it fhould ftop. To overcome this evil, *i. e.* the difeafe, without injuring the conftitution, and leaving other complaints as the confequence of their exhibition, lies the difficulty. Here, then, we fee the neceffity of much ftudy, and no lefs experience, before we take on us the important office of regulating health.

BUT,

BUT, to return; with refpect to the ufe of mercury, in the difeafe which is the fubject of thefe pages, an inftance might be adduced, which is given me on good authority, where much mifchief has been occafioned by throwing it into the habit, and carrying it to too great a length, under the idea of a prophylactic. The perfon alluded to was bit by a dog; this medicine was exhibited; the confequence, as I am informed, is, fuch a ftate of debility, as will take a long time, and much circumfpection in the phyfician, to remove.

THE limits we wifh to prefcribe to ourfelves, will not allow us to enter farther on the fubject of fpecifics, elfe much might be faid to prove, that all hitherto known have but little claim to infallibility in removing, or preventing Hydrophobia.

SOME, we muft obferve, from a peculiarity of conftitution, never are affected with

Hydro-

Hydrophobia, though really bit by a rabid animal.* Or the body may happen to be in such a state at the time of the bite, that it becomes able to resist the powers of the poison. We know, that for the reception of several of those poisons that produce disease, especially the class of fevers from infection, when the body is predisposed for their reception, they become more readily infectious, and the more readily exert their force. If the body be in a more tonic state, and not thus predisposed by any debilitating causes, rendering it more than commonly irritable, the poison seldomer takes effect. And hence it comes to pass, that the same poisons of the same strength, acting chiefly upon the nervous system, shall produce, or not produce their peculiar effects, according to the state of the body at the time of their reception.

WHEN

---

* Dr. Vaughan relates, that between twenty and thirty were bit by a mad dog, and only the one whose case he lays before the public was affected.

WHEN one of thefe poifons is received, we fhall fuppofe it that of a rabid animal, and it either meets with this peculiarity of conftitution, or with a body not predifpofed eafily to receive it, by which means the perfon efcapes the infection; fhould fome of thefe fpecifics be adminiftered, it will be affirmed, the efcape was to be attributed to the noftrum. And I have little fcruple in declaring my belief, that many a fpecific owes its reputation folely to this circumftance, not to any virtues it poffeffes in deftroying the poifon.

WE find the fame peculiarity of conftitution, of which we have been treating, refift the variolous virus. Many have been repeatedly inoculated for the fmall-pox, without effect — Others have purpofely frequented the company of perfons in the difeafe, with a defire to catch it, but in vain. To enquire into what this peculiarity confifts, is foreign to our prefent pur-

M   pofe :

pofe : it is enough for us to know the fact; and is fuch as feveral of my readers, no doubt, have themfelves obferved.

THE faliva of a rabid animal appears to me to be among the weaker poifons, and, for the moft part, to require a length of time to fhew its effects, greater than any other with which we are acquainted. From this caufe it is, then, that fo few of thofe that are bit, become infected. This is a wife precaution of the Creator, for our good, fince its effects, when the poifon does take place, are fo dreadful, and fo much removed beyond the power of medicine, as far as we have yet been able to difcover.

A MAN bit by a mad cat did not become hydrophobic till the following May, which was between the eighth and ninth month after the accident.* But this, we own, very rarely happens. We have a fecond example, where

* Vand. Wiefel Obf. Rar. Cent. I. No. 100. p. 400.

where the perſon was bit in December, and did not become hydrophobic, till the beginning of the following May : this was about five months after the accident. And even a third caſe is taken notice of by Van Swieten, where the effects did not take place, till after five months and eleven days.

SOME are alſo bit through various thick ſubſtances, as folds of cloth ; ſtockings ; gloves ; perhaps even boots. Here the teeth of the animal muſt have been ſo clean wiped, that no ſaliva adheres to them, and, conſequently, no infection can be communicated. This is another caſe in which, if ſpecifics ſhould have been adminiſtered, they would have obtained a degree of credit, which they by no means deſerved.

WHEN perſons, however, are bit in this manner, to know that the danger is leſs, may relieve their minds from much anxiety, and from the miſery always created by apprehenſion. Yet, though much be in favour

of

of non-infection in thefe circumftances, I would not wifh, by what I have faid, to give a fatal fecurity. It will ftill be fafe to act as if we thought the poifon would ap-pear, and either extirpate, or have recourfe to fome of thofe means already recommended.

THOUGH I have thus been ufing endea-vours to difuade from a reliance on noftrums, yet it is not wantonly done. Few men, I am confident, can take pleafure in deceiv-ing; and few would wifh to take away that fupport of hope the miferable lean on, did they not forefee that this fecurity drew after it fatal confequences. Men of undoubted profeffional knowledge, candour, and hu-manity, have of late ftood forth to deftroy this ill-placed confidence. But it is from a thorough conviction of the inefficacy of fuch means, joined to an ardent zeal for the fake of truth; and when I follow their footfteps, and endeavour farther to enforce their doctrine, it is folely with the fame view.

A QUES-

A QUESTION of no fmall magnitude, in my opinion, comes next to be difcuffed, *i. e.* at what diftance of time from the bite may all dread and apprehenfion of danger be laid afide? This may be difficult to determine with certainty. We have already taken notice of the difference of conftitutions, and the varied degree of virulency of the poifon in propagating the difeafe, and determining the time. But I am inclined to believe, that the period of its appearance is not fo diftant from that of the bite, nor fo indi-termined, as fome have fuppofed.

IT appears to me extremely doubtful, whether it ever fhews itfelf after lying latent for feveral years, as fome cafes of which we read would perfuade us. I am not without fufpicions relative to their authenticity. I do not at prefent recol-lect any on which I can confide, where it fhewed itfelf at a later period than on the nineteenth month, and this only in

one

one cafe;* and, till I find more reafon to change my opinion, I hold, that all fear and apprehenfion may ceafe after one year, or fifteen months at fartheft; perhaps I might mention a much earlier period.

THE man bit by a mad cat, as related in the Oferv. Rarior. Cent. 1. No. 100. p. 400, became hydrophobic on the following May, i. e. between the eighth and ninth month after.

ANOTHER cafe is given, of a perfon bit in December, and who, in May following, became hydrophobic, i. e. about five months afterwards.

VAN SWIETEN relates another, where the effects appeared at the end of five months and eleven days.

MR.

---

* I am not without fufpicions of the authenticity even of this cafe. Mr. Hunter writes me—" The " greateft diftance we have yet affertained is eleven " months:" and adds, " I cannot fuppofe, that the " time is fo vague as is advanced."—Letter to the author.

Mr. Charles Belamy was bit on the 14th of February; about the middle of April he felt a pain in the part, refembling the rheumatifm, which he had experienced for two or three years before. On the 7th of June following, he took fome pills for it.—On the 13th he felt a contraction of the fcrotum, a fymptom often found on the approach of Hydrophobia—on the 17th he died.—This was five months after the accident.

Abraham Palmer was bit on the 9th of June, 1783.—On the 17th of July he came to the hofpital, with fymptoms of the difeafe.—He died on the third day after.

John Brown was bit in the beginning of January.—On the 30th of April following, i. e. three months after, he came to the London hofpital.—He died the fame day.

The

THE gardener's fervant, who was bit the fame evening with John Brown, continued well till the 28th of April; or, in other words, was affected two days fooner.—He died the 1ft of May.

THE old man of fixty-nine, bit alfo on the fame evening, by the fame dog, became affected about twenty-fix days after: but it was twelve days from this till he died; or, about five weeks from the time of the bite.

MASTER R. was bit on the 5th of December, 1784.—He continued without any fymptoms of difeafe till the 11th of January following.—On the 13th he died.

THE poor French woman, who was bit by the fame dog a few minutes before, remained well till Friday the 16th of March, and died hydrophobic on the Tuefday following, at Two o'clock in the morning,*

i. e.

---

* Mr. Hunter's fubfequent letter to the author.

i. e. three months and eleven days after the bite.

THE girl Chrifty, who was brought to the Edinburgh Royal Infirmary in 1765, continued well till within a day or two before fhe came there, which was five weeks from the bite.—She died on the fecond day after.

THE boy whofe cafe is related by Dr. Mead in the Philofophical Tranfactions, was bit on the 20th of April.—On the 22d of May he became affected.—He died on the 24th, *i. e.* two days after.

A SECOND patient under Dr. Mead's care, aged forty-five, was bit ten weeks before he faw him, which was on the 11th of November.—He died the fame day; but, we muft obferve, he became affected on the 8th, *i. e.* three days before.

N   IN

IN a third patient's cafe, with which the Doctor favours us, the fymptoms began to difcover themfelves on the third month after the accident.—He continued three days under Hydrophobia before he died.

DR. MUNCKLEY's patient [vid. Med. Tranf.] was bit on the 11th of July, 1760.—On the 19th of Auguft he felt a difficulty of fwallowing—on the 21ft he died.

JAMES PATTON was bit on the 18th of November, 1774.*—On the 9th of February following he became affected, i. e. very near three months after; and on the 12th, i. e. three days from this, he died.

IN one of the cafes related by Dr. Vaughan, the fymptoms began to appear about a month after the bite.†

IN

---

* Med. Comm.

† Both the fea-bath and the Ormfkirk medicine were ufed here.

IN a fecond cafe, by the fame author, the fymptoms did not fhew themfelves till nine months from the bite.

A THIRD was attacked with Hydrophobia in the fpace of a month after.

OF three cafes related by Hildanus, two of the patients became affected at the end of three months; the third, at feven.

DR. LISTER's patient fell ill five weeks after the bite.

DR. HAMMOND's became hydrophobic in fix.

WILLIAM BLAND, near Daventry, who was Dr. Adams's patient, became affected four months after.

THE only patient of the nine, who were bit in prifon by the fame mad wolf, and

who

who became affected, died hydrophobic on
the fourth month after the accident.*

THE patient alluded to, as related in the
fifth volume of the Edinburgh Essays, said
to be affected, when bit, by a venereal complaint, died hydrophobic in the space of a
month after.

DR. BERKENHAUT's patient was bit
by one of his father's hounds, six or seven
weeks before he saw him, which was at ten
in the morning.—He died hydrophobic at
twelve the same evening.

MR. NOURSE gives us a case in the Philo-
sophical Transactions, of rabies, where the
patient was not affected till nineteen months
after: he then died hydrophobic.—This is
the boy, of whom it is said, that between
the bite and his death, he was cut for the
stone, and recovered.—This case runs to a
later period than what we mentioned; but
those

---

* Vid. Lond. Med. Journ. Vol. V.

thofe from four weeks to three months, are, by much, the moft frequent.

WILLIAM KNIPE, a farmer, near Kirby Stephen, remained in health after he was bit, as the account before me fays, till about the eleventh month.—This is likewife a later period than, for the moft part, we find, takes place.*

CÆLIUS

---

* In the Whitehall Evening Poft for Feb. 12, 1785, we have the following relation :—" About eleven " months ago, William Knipe, a farmer, near Kirby " Stephen, was alarmed in bed by a noife in his byre; " when he lighted a candle, and went in, and found a " cow of his in fierce conteft with a fox.—He at- " tempted to feize the fox, and received a very fevere " bite in his hand.—After three weeks, the cow, fome " fwine, and feveral other animals which had been bit " by it, became mad, which alarmed him much; and " he went to Ormfkirk, and took the medicine.—Till " Monday fe'nnight he felt no inconvenience from the " bite; when, in Kirby Stephen market, he com- " plained of a pain, from the wounded hand up to his " fhoulder, and went home.—On that evening the " Hydrophobia took place, which held him, at in- " tervals; and on the Thurfday following he died " raving mad."—Here, then, is another cafe of the failure of the celebrated Ormfkirk medicine.

CÆLIUS AURELIANUS places the period of attack at forty days. Galen is much of the fame opinion ; as are likewife Paulus and Actuarius.

CHOISEL's patients died hydrophobic in thirty-three days.—Speaking on the fubject of bathing, and reprobating the practice, he fays, " Not one of thofe who depended " folely on this remedy, furvived the bite " more than thirty-three days."

ON the whole, from thefe now mentioned, without troubling the reader with any more, I am authorized, I think, to fay, that if a period, fuch as I have already ventured to name, elapfes, and no fymptoms appear, apprehenfions of danger may, with reafon, be laid afide.

BOOKS have told, and tradition has kept it alive, that the poifon may remain latent for years, and may appear at any time after.
This

This notion multiplies fears, and magnifies the idea of danger to fuch a degree, as to imbitter the whole period of life : this, furely, is a great evil.

As an example, the reader may take that of a perfon in this place.* The ftory is told me by a gentleman whofe authority I cannot difpute, from his opportunities of knowing.

THE gentleman, it feems, was bit by a dog that he apprehended to be mad. Fear feized him for the confequences. It hung on his mind, and clouded every enjoyment. And though he lived upwards of twelve years after, without experiencing any injury from the bite, yet he was not able to throw his fears afide. It was his conftant requeft to his family and friends, all this time, that if he went mad, he might not be fmothered between two beds, but be bled to death in his own garden.—We have little reafon to doubt, but many others have laboured un-

der

* IPSWICH.

der the fame fears, equally groundlefs, from a fimilar caufe.

IT is my wifh, then, to point out the fallacy, as it appears to me, of this doctrine, and render confidence to any of my fellow-creatures thus unfortunately circumftanced, in the hopes of their fecurity, after a deter-mined time, which, from the cafes collated, I have marked as already mentioned.

THE difeafe itfelf, which is the confe-quence of the bite, comes next to be con-fidered. This we fhall not promife to do at any great length; as it has already been well defcribed by feveral ingenious and learned authors, and as little is left to add to the defcriptions they have given us.

WE fhall pafs over all the difputes re-lative to the antiquity of the difeafe.—It is of little moment, whether it appeared in the days of Afclepiades, as Le Clerc alledges; or was known in the time of Homer, as
Cælius

Cælius Aurelianus labours, by quotations from the Iliad, to prove.

It feems fuperfluous, likewife, to run over all the variety of fymptoms that we find mentioned in different cafes, when this dreadful malady manifefts itfelf. They are various in various fubjects; perhaps diverfified chiefly by the difference of conftitution, the age, and the habit at the time. This, we likewife find, is the cafe in other difeafes. The pathognomonic, and peculiar fymptoms, whereby it is diftinguifhed from others, are but few.

The Hydrophobia, or *aquæ pavor* (dread of liquids) has been held, by fome, as its characteriftic mark: by others, it has been refufed, and examples quoted to fupport this opinion. This, on the authority of feveral authors, I likewife, till of late, doubted; and thought with them, for that reafon, the name, Hydrophobia, improper. Names, however, do not change things;

O   and

and fince we find a difficulty of fwallowing, with a horror at the approach of liquids to the lips, or when they touch the *gula*, a conftant attendant, we cannot be wrong in giving this as one of the chief diftinguifhing fymptoms of the complaint.

WE fee a dread of water, it is true, attend fome other difeafes :—the patients refufe, peremptorily refufe, to take liquids. But, I believe, from a comparifon of thefe with thofe from the bite of a rabid animal, a material difference fhall be difcovered. I have converfed with many who have attended the complaints : I have feen one which I fhall ever remember, though, at that time, I had no medical reading, nor for feveral years after, being then a boy, which has left fuch an impreffion on my mind as can never be obliterated.—The horrors, the tremors, the convulfions of the breaft, throat, eyes, and the whole upper parts of the body, at the approach of the cup—the hafty manner its contents are thrown into

the

the mouth, when the patient has refolution enough to attempt to fwallow, with the fcene that immediately follows; are fuch, as, I am perfuaded, have, in no other dif- eafe, faid to have an *aquæ pavor*, any exift- ence :—and I am confirmed herein by the teftimony of many with whom I have con- verfed, and whofe experience in it gives them a right to decide.

I. The firft fymptom is generally a pain in the part where the bite has been received, ftretching in the courfe of the lymphatics towards the heart, or where they unite with the fanguiferous fyftem. We might quote many examples to prove this; but, we ap- prehend, it will be thought fuperfluous.

Then come laffitude; inactivity, and torpidnefs; fenfation of a weight; dif- turbed fleep (fometimes none at all till death clofes the fcene); terrifying dreams; convulfions; ftarting of the tendons; per-
petual

petual reſtleſſneſs; ſighing; dejectedneſs;*
with a deſire of ſolitude.—External organs
of ſenſation extremely ſenſible; the ſmalleſt
motion of the air producing moſt painful
ſenſations; the light offenſive to the ſight;
great thirſt; tongue dry; eyes quick and
penetrating, with ſomething not eaſily expreſſed in the countenance, yet is what cannot be miſtaken, and which differs from the
appearance of the countenance in all other
complaints.† Cannot bear a recumbent
poſture; cannot bear to look at any tranſ-
parent body, ſuch as a looking glaſs;‡ cannot bear a perſon in ſcarlet clothes—or in
white

---

* "Whatever he wanted to obtain, whether to
" have ſome diſagreeable object removed, or ſome re-
" queſt granted, it was implored in the moſt piteous
" manner."—Dr. Vaughan.

† " The ſingular appearance of his eyes, was very
" ſtriking; and is, I believe, peculiar to people la-
" bouring under the Hydrophobia.—The iris ſome-
" times changes to an orange colour."—Dr. Vaughan.

‡ " He could look at his own urine in a dark co-
" loured chamber-pot, but could not when put into
" a glaſs."—Dr. Vaughan.

white clothes.—Pulfe unfteady, and rather hard; changing frequently; fometimes every minute.—Afpect likewife various, which is eafily obferved, by different changes, even while one converfes with the patient.*—Urine fmall quantity.

II. Second.—The pain in the bitten part now vanifhes; mufcles of the *gula* now convulfed, as foon as water or other liquids touch them, producing the utmoft uneafinefs in fwallowing; a great fenfe of fuffocation; pain about the *cartilago enfi-formis*; fenfe of a boiling heat in the fto-mach; ftrong palpitations of the heart; unufual titilation of the urethra; urine forcibly expelled by fpafms; with *fcroti, et penis contractio fpaftica,* to a degree of great pain; after making water, *feminis emiffio.*† Great dilatation of the pupil; blind-

---

* Dr. Fothergill.

† Both Mead and Lifter, as well as later authors, take notice of the *venetri frequens erectio cum feminis in-voluntarii*

blindnefs, fometimes temporary only; fometimes for two or three days; fometimes con-
tinual: and this of either one or of both
eyes. Copious flow of vifcid faliva.—Reachings to vomit—not always vomiting—yet
often regurgitations of the ftomach.—The
fpafms of the cremafter mufcle at length
ceafe; at length the eyes lofe their fierce,
threatening appearance, and become more
fixed.

As the difeafe advances, the pain from
fwallowing encreafes; and liquids are totally

---

voluntarii jactu—as alfo Cælius Aurelianus. Van Swieten likewife relates more than one inftance of it:
among others, he mentions the cafe of a porter, as
given by Hermandes in his Thefaurus, who breathed
out his foul, as it is there expreffed, for the laft three
days of his life, in this way; and, in Bonetus's Sepul-
chra Anatomica, the cafe of an old man of feventy is
mentioned, who, from the priapifm that attended the
difeafe, was urged to converfe with his wife. It is
obferved, however, that fome of thofe faid to be fo affected, had large blifters on them at the time; and it
may, in part, perhaps, be attributed to the irritation
given by them—yet, only in part, as we fo frequently
find it where none have been applied.

tally refufed.—Hands and feet become cold : pulfe intermits, and is irregular.—The paroxifms of the convulfions return at fhorter intervals—are more violent.—Now a conftant talking—yet, when queftions are afked, rational anfwers are received from the affected. —Pulfe now becomes more frequent.—At length conftant delirium—horror—and extreme anxiety.—Sometimes, in the fits, a defire to bite ; but, for the moft part, none. —*Rifus fardonicus.*—Spafmodic affections ftill encreafe, and become fo ftrong as to tofs the patient out of bed, if not forcibly held in it.—Death.—This takes place varioufly—not unfrequently as if ftrangled with a cord ; fometimes placidly, and without the leaft ftruggle ; and, fometimes, even with a fmile on the countenance.*

FROM

---

* —" He fell back in the bed, and died with a " countenance as much oppofed to that of the minute " before as it is poffible to conceive ; the fcene being " clofed with feveral of the moft beautiful fmiles."— Mr. Babington, on Palmer's cafe.

☞ Vid. cafes in the appendix for a proof of the fymptoms.

FROM the firft appearance of Hydrophobia, till death finifhes the patient's miferies, at a medium, it is about three days.* In one of the foregoing cafes, we found it continue twelve days; but this is a rare occurrence.

MR. BELLAMY became affected with the firft fymptoms on the 13th.—He died on the 17th—*i. e.* on the fourth day.

ABRAHAM PALMER felt fome fymptoms on the 17th.—He died on the third day after.

JOHN BROWN fell ill on the 30th.—He was brought to the London hofpital on Monday, May 4th.—He died the fame night at eleven o'clock.

THE

---

* Dr. Boerhaave places the final period of the Hydrophobia on the fourth day; Dr. Mead, on the fecond. Perhaps, on an average, we fhall be nearer the truth by faying, that the third day from the firft fymptoms of the difeafe, is that which clofes the melancholy cataftrophe.

THE gardener's fervant continued well till the 28th of April.—He died on the 1ft of May, at noon.

THE old man (Bean) of fixty-nine, continued twelve days, as already taken notice of.

MASTER R. became affected on the 11th.—He died on the 13th.

THE poor French woman grew ill on Friday the 16th.—She died on Tuefday following, at two in the morning.

CHRISTY came to the Edinburgh infirmary ill.—She died on the fecond day after.

DR. MEAD's firft patient became affected on the 22d of May.—He died on the 24th, —i. e. two days after.

P   HIS

His second patient became affected on the 8th.—He died on the 11th,—*i. e.* three days after.

His third patient continued three days from the time he was affected.

Dr. Munckley's patient grew ill on the 19th.—On the 21ft he died,—*i. e.* on the third day after.

James Patton became affected on the 9th of February, and died on the 12th,—*i. e.* three days after.

William Knipe felt himself ill on Monday, when at Market.—He died on Thurfday following.

Dr. Vaughan's firft patient began to complain on Sunday evening.—He died on Wednefday morning.

His

His fecond patient became firft affected on Tuefday June 6th, in the afternoon.— He died about ten o'clock on Thurfday evening.

His third patient began to complain on the 28th of Auguft, about noon.—He died four days after.

The period which the difeafe takes to finifh its career, feems to be nearly the fame in the human, and in the inferior animals.

It would appear, however, that the virus takes lefs time to become active in the canine tribe than in the human race.

We find the hydrophobic fymptoms made their appearance in a dog, bit at the fame time with John Brown, the gardener's fervant, and the old man Bean, about the feventh day after.

In

In several other cases we might quote, where animals were bit, the symptoms came on in the space of three weeks.

From the symptoms of Hydrophobia now enumerated, it is evident, beyond a possibility of doubt, that the disease belongs to the spasmodic class. That the affection begins first in the part bit; then proceeds to the throat, and other parts of the body, most of which are, perhaps, affected by sympathy, and consent. We find the stomach, the fauces, external and internal, and the *scorbiculus cordis*, affected in a special manner with a preternatural sensibility. The diaphragm is convulsed; the abdominal muscles are forcibly contracted; hence proceeds the involuntary expulsion of the urine sometimes observable. The priapism likewise, and affection of the cremaster, occur where no blisters have been applied to the body; though, on other occasions, this symptom has been attributed to them.

BOER-

BOERHAAVE muft undoubtedly be wrong, when he calls the difeafe *Summè Inflammatorius*: for, furely, neither the fymptoms, nor the diffections of fuch as have died in confequence of the bite of a rabid animal, in the leaft, authorize us to draw this conclufion. On the contrary, if we confider the fymptoms as related by all who have had opportunities of feeing genuine hydrophobia, it muft appear evident, that the difeafe is as truly fpafmodic, as any to which the human body is liable.

IF this be allowed, an indication of cure immediately prefents itfelf. The firft thing, without doubt, we are to attempt, is, to allay the inordinate affection of thefe parts. If there be any cure, it muft proceed in this line. Here, however, all practitioners have found infuperable difficulties. The time for acting is fhort; the difeafe runs its courfe moft rapidly; while the fymptoms every moment encreafe in violence. The

avenues,

avenues, through which we might expect
to combat it, are, almost at once, shut up.
The patient can neither swallow food, nor
medicine. Yet, let us endeavour to act,
and to act also with vigour, while the least
possibility remains. It would be cruel—it
would be inhuman, to forsake the patient
under these melancholy circumstances.

In most of the cases I have perused, where
I consider the disease really had been present,
and where the warm bath had been tried, I
find it a remedy that gives the greatest, and
most speedy relief. All express the comfort
they receive from it; and, notwithstanding
the reluctance with which they enter, and
the horror produced from the very touch
of the water, which seems to arise from a
morbid sensibility of the nervous system in
general, and of the nerves of the cuticle in
particular, the benefit and ease they experience, give them courage a second time
to surmount the dread they feel, and go
into it in hopes of similar relief.

WE

We find, that after coming out of it they fwallow with more eafe; and now is the time to adminifter both food and medicine. One of our chief endeavours fhould be to protract the difeafe, and gain as much time as poffible for farther action. And this feems to be beft done by keeping up the patient's ftrength. Hence the propriety of fome eafy digefted aliment; and if this cannot be adminiftered by the mouth, nutritive clyfters muft be had recourfe to as a fubftitute.

Antispasmodics, of the ftrongeft nature, fhould be applied externally to the throat, and given in as large quantities internally as poffible. If we give opiates with the hopes of inducing fleep, we fhould remember, that as the difeafe is violent, the dofe fhould be in proportion. We are not to trifle away a moment of our time. It it is now moft precious. Six or eight times the common quantity may be adminiftered

at

at once; and repeated after some interval, if we find the intention not yet answered.

THOSE who are acquainted with the doses of this medicine that have been exhibited in some other violent spasmodic affections, as the locked jaw (trismus) tetanus, and a few others of this class, with safety and the happiest effects, will not censure this opinion.

As we wish our medicine to produce its effects in the shortest space of time possible, we must make choice of the fittest form for this purpose. Hence pills are exceptionable, because they do not dissolve, or diffuse themselves speedily enough; and liquid forms, if it be at all practicable to employ them, are to be preferred. But the irritability of the fauces, highly beyond what we experience in any other disease, and which hardly admits even of the touch of a fluid of any kind, opposes here, most powerfully, our endeavours. I say the irritability of

the

the fauces ; for, if the fubftance could but get into the œfophagus, experience points out, that deglutition, or the pufhing, by the force and contraction of the mufcles of thefe parts, the fubftance into the ftomach, is performed with little or no inconvenience.*

Q . FROM

---

* " It was curious to obferve, what pains he took
" to fwallow the medicine, and what perfeverance he
" fhewed in getting it into the œfophagus. He fixed
" his eyes ftedfaftly upon it [Mufk fcr. j Extr. Theb.
" gr. ij in a bolus] for fome time, and having applied
" it to his mouth, he crammed it as far back into the
" fauces as he could reach, which feemed to be the
" fuperior part of the gullet ; after which, deglutition
" was performed with little or no difficulty.—This
" lack of difficulty in fwallowing, when the fubftance
" was conveyed into the œfophagus, I defired fome
" of the faculty who were prefent, to remark ; as it
" contradicted an opinion univerfally received, refpect-
" ing the diforder."—Dr. Vaughan. Cafe I. p. 7.

—" He could chew bread ; but feemed very atten-
" tive in keeping it from touching the back part of the
" fauces ; and, whenever he attempted to fwallow it,
" the fame fymptoms were brought on that enfued
" from his feeing water (but in a lefs degree) until he
" had got the fubftance into the œfophagus, when it
" was

FROM the cafes on record it appears, that the region of the ftomach is much affected. We find a boiling heat, as it is expreffed, at the pit of the ftomach, in thofe Dr. Vaughan

---

" was tranfmitted to the ftomach without difficulty."
—Dr. Vaughan. Cafe II. p. 24.

—" It is generally believed," fays this author, in his remarks on the difeafe, fubjoined to the cafe, " that " a confiderable difficulty in fwallowing is joined to " the dread of water ; and that the œfophagus, with " the mufcles fubfervient to deglutition, are efpecially " concerned in this difeafe. The attentive obferver " will find the matter mifreprefented : the principal " foundation of the evil feems to reft upon a *morbid* " *fenfibility* both of the *external* and *internal fauces.* For, " the fight of a liquid, or the application of any fub- " ftance to the internal fauces, but more efpecially of " a fluid, inftantly excites the moft painful feelings. " Nay, the fame fymptoms are produced by touching " the *external fauces* with a fluid; or by the contact of " cold air with thefe parts ; and nearly in as great a " degree. But a folid, or a fluid fubftance being con- " veyed into the œfophagus, the tranfit into the fto- " mach is accomplifhed with little or no impediment : " fo that, in fact, the difficulty is furmounted before " the patient is engaged in the action of fwallowing."
—Dr. Vaughan. p. 46.

Vaughan attended; a symptom that produced great uneasiness, and proves this viscus to have been affected. From this, and the large quantities of viscid saliva secreted in the last period of the disease, a quantity of which must necessarily pass down the œsophagus, notwithstanding the efforts made to eject it by the mouth, the stomach must be rendered more irritable. This cannot fail to prove another great obstacle to the internal use of medicine. The vomiting so frequently observed, must, I apprehend, proceed, in a certain degree, from this vitiated secretion, in addition to the irritability mentioned.

If we attend to the laws of derivation, and retain a belief, that the encrease of certain discharges, will produce the diminution of others, we may find a second indication; which is to endeavour to open the perspirable pores, and excite sweat. This, if brought about, which will likewise have its difficulties, may dissipate, perhaps, some

of

of the poifon, and leſſen the inordinate action of the ſalivary glands. It is alſo well
known to be powerfully antiſpaſmodic.

THE ſkin would appear to be the natural
emunctory of many of the violent poifons
producing diſeaſes. We find it ſo of the
ſmall-pox; the meaſles; the poifon that
produces the white miliary eruption; the
poifon that excites the ſcarlet effloreſ-
cence in the diſeaſe named the *Scarlatina
Anginoſa,* and a few others. If we may
be allowed to reaſon from analogy in this
caſe, it would appear, that theſe analogies
are not unnatural.

MEDICINES, properly choſen, ſhould co-
operate with the warm bath; and a proper
attention ſhould, at the ſame time, be paid
to the other natural diſcharges, I mean
urine and ſtools. For the one, perhaps,
clyſters will be ſufficient; for the other, if
occaſion requires, we muſt have recourſe to
thoſe articles of the *materia medica* adapted

to

to the purpofe, and known to every prac-
titioner.

How far bleeding is indicated I dare not
venture to fay. Dr. Fothergill, and other
eminent practitioners, ufed it with freedom.
It is alfo powerfully antifpafmodic; but it
is, at the fame time, powerfully debilitating.
Here, then, feems to be as much againft it,
as for it; and the pro and con fo equally
poized, that we are at fome lofs which fide
to efpoufe.

To leffen inflammation is out of the
queftion. We have feen, from the fymptoms, there is almoft none: diffections
confirm it ftill farther: nor does a hard
pulfe at all times indicate V. S. Irritation
(and it is here of the moft forcible kind)
will give a ftrong degree of vibration to
an artery. A proof that the pulfe is affected by irritaton is, its frequent and almoft momentary change from foft to hard;
feeble to ftrong. From the violent degree
of

of excitement in the brain, patients bear
bleeding, however, to a greater quantity,
without fainting, than in moſt other diſeaſes. Doctor Fothergill directs them to
be bled ſtanding, as they will faint the rea-
dier, an indication, with him, to deſiſt.—
I dare determine nothing in ſo critical and
nice a point. I muſt leave it to thoſe of
greater diſcernment, whether it is to be
done at all, or how far it ought to be pro-
ſecuted.

Blistering certainly is more eaſily
determined. Its uſe is indicated in almoſt
all ſpaſmodic diſeaſes. It ſeldom, if ever,
produces debility; and it often removes
irregularity in the diſtribution of the fluids,
&c. But it acts, perhaps, too ſlow in this
caſe. We cannot have its effects in leſs
than ſeveral hours: nor fully, perhaps, in
leſs than from twelve to twenty-four; and,
in this time, the diſeaſe may have arrived
at its utmoſt extreme. I ſhould not, however, heſitate to apply them over the whole
                                        ſcalp,

fcalp, and to the nape of the neck. I am doubtful whether we fhould blifter the throat, as it might prevent our ufe of ftronger antifpafmodics. Here, too, it will require fegacity to determine. The comparative power of thefe muft be carefully weighed, that we may not trifle, and the practice commence accordingly.

To adminifter mercury now, I am fully perfuaded, will prove ufelefs. Let us remember the fhort period that is allowed for life, from the commencement of the hydrophobic fymptoms. We cannot raife a falivation, and obtain its effects, in fo fhort a time as two, three, or four days. Befides, in all the cafes in which it has been tried, either as a preventative, or for a cure of Hydrophobia, we have already endeavoured to make it appear, that it has failed of fuccefs. If we are to be guided by reafon, by the pathology of the difeafe, our chief, and fole hope feems evidently placed in antifpafmodics. Mufk, caftor, camphor, opiates,

ates, zinc, preparations of copper, and such like, ought, then, to be adminiftered. The moft powerful fhould be applied firft, to obviate, if poffible, that violence, which otherwife muft fpeedily be expected.

I HAVE no new remedy to propofe. No boafted fpecific to amufe the reader with. In place thereof, I have endeavoured, and I think, on good grounds, to fhake his be-lief in all fuch panaceas; the *inanis jactan-tia multorum fpecificorum*, as Boerhaave juftly ftiles them; and to awaken the patient to a fenfe of his duty for the prefervation of his life, while there is an opportunity for it. If his credulity is removed, he has it in his power to apply what reafon points out for his fafety, and experience, in many well authenticated cafes, confirms to be effectual.

HE deferves, we think, fome credit, who points out a defect, though he may not be able to fupply it. To be fenfible of

our

our ignorance, to be convinced we have hitherto acted wrong, is one step towards acting right, and towards knowledge, since we then, and not before, turn our thoughts to another direction in search of it. He that can remove an error in so essential a point as this we have been considering, though he may not be able to supply a remedy, may thus be the indirect agent of its accomplishment, in as far as it opens a field for investigators of greater capacity, who may be more fortunate in their researches.

NOTHING is so fatal in medicine as a blind security. Nor should we pronounce any species of disease absolutely incurable. All we have a right to say is, that we cannot accomplish it. For, though the present, and antecedent ages have failed in finding a remedy, we act rashly in concluding the same of succeeding generations. The mind is progressive, and the knowledge of one link in the great chain of causes and effects, serves as a key to the next; this,

R   again,

again, to another; and so on. A disease may arrive to such a point, that from viewing the ravages it has already made in various parts of the machine, and the comparative strength of the whole, we may justly, and with little hesitation, conclude it incurable in that particular individual; but, at a certain time of the disease, our conclusions ought to have been very different.

I AM unwilling to call any disease, to which the human body is liable, not even Hydrophobia itself, absolutely beyond the reach of medicine. This notion would encrease indolence, idleness, and put a fatal stop to an industrious search after knowledge.

I MAY, however, venture to give it as my own opinion, that no real case of Hydrophobia, well authenticated, has to this day ever been cured. I read of many cures, but I doubt the authenticity of them—*i. e.*

I doubt,

I doubt, whether the difeafe arifing from the bite of a rabid animal really exifted in thofe perfons, on whom the cures are faid to be performed.

WE all know the power of the imagination over the funćtions of the body. We all know the effećts of fear. If a bite from an animal, fufpećted to be mad, is received, it inftantly awakens apprehenfion for the confequences. This difturbs the mind, and induces a train of fymptoms, in many refpećts refembling what would have really taken place, was the true difeafe prefent.

ONE of the moft noted cures we have on record appears to me to be that related by Doćtor Nugent of Bath, on which he built an ingenious treatife, at one time confiderably read.—His patient's name was Elizabeth Briant. And even here, I think, from a careful perufal of the cafe, it may be difcovered, that imagination, and an apprehenfion of danger, formed the chief of

the

the symptoms which the Doctor attributed to real Hydrophobia.

FROM the time her apothecary advised her to use prophylactics, and go into the cold bath, which was a fortnight after the accident, we find her under confiderable agitation of mind. We cannot doubt of her apprehenfions being raifed by his fug-geftions. Thefe encreafed, till Hydropho-bia, it is faid, actually appeared. She trem-bled at the very fight of a dog; nor could she touch one without the greateft emotion. The Doctor tells us she was well, and could again fwallow, and continued well for fome time, till a perfon came and told her, that, though she thought herfelf cured, she might be fure to die, and defired her not to feed herfelf with vain hopes of an efcape. At this, as might be expected, she was greatly moved; and, inftantly, all her fymptoms returned as violent as before; nor was it without much care, and the exhibition of the fame antifpafmodics, that they were re-

removed.—She muſt, by this alarm, have been thrown into violent hyſterics, and, no doubt, had both a dread of liquids, and difficulty of ſwallowing, ſymptoms which this *proti*-form diſeaſe may, and has, oc-caſionally, put on.

THE Doctor ſeems, however, to have followed a judicious enough plan of cure. —He ſaw her diſeaſe was to be ranked among the ſpaſmodic claſs; he therefore adminiſtered the moſt powerful antiſpaſ-modics internally, and applied them exter-nally.—He purſued his plan; kept her mind as much at eaſe as poſſible, and ſuc-ceeded in reſtoring her to health. She was ſeized, indeed, on the thirty-ſecond day after the bite, which is much about the common time when ſymptoms of Hydro-phobia firſt ſhew themſelves; but, it was not till after being alarmed at a dog's going mad, that was bit by the ſame animal which bit her.

In

In a cafe, called Canine Madnefs, treated
fuccefsfully by M. Wrightfon [vid. Med.
Tranf.] the difeafe made its appearance
much earlier than we generally find. The
boy (Thomas Agar) was bit on the Sunday;
on Tuefday the dog was hanged, it is added,
with all the fymptoms of madnefs on him.
—Next day, *i. e.* Wednefday, fymptoms of
Hydrophobia, we are told, appeared in the
boy.—On Friday, when Mr. Wrightfon
firft faw him, he was tied down to the bed
with cords.—The fymptoms related feem
more like phrenzy, than Hydrophobia; and,
from their commencing fo early, it inclines
me to think, they proceeded entirely from
fear. We have few cafes of true Hydrophobia on record, where the fymptoms
fhewed themfelves at an earlier period than
five weeks.—Mr. Wrightfon informs us,
he purfued Dr. Nugent's Method of cure,
viz. the exhibition of antifpafmodics, as
mufk, opium, V. S. and the like.

In

IN another cafe, related by Mr. Falkener [vid. Med. Tranf.] where the difeafe was alfo faid to be prefent, Hannah Moore, which was the woman's name that was bit, felt no inconvenience, till two horfes, bit by the fame dog, fell ill and died.—All the dogs bit by this mad animal were then hanged.—Thefe things could not fail to alarm her greatly. We are not told at what diftance this was from the bite; but a train of fymptoms are given, refembling Hydrophobia, and a method of treatment, which proved fuccefsful, added.

A GENTLEMAN of veracity informs me of a perfon bit by a dog, and who, from terror and apprehenfion left he fhould become affected with Hydrophobia, though he had no certainty of the dog's madnefs, really grew ill, and believed himfelf already under the difeafe. A Phyfician of character was fent for; this was even fome weeks after the accident. When he arrived, he found

found the patient affected with fymptoms, which a fuperficial obferver would immediately have called hydrophobic. He treated the cafe as a nervous affection, ufing, at the fame time, arguments to confirm the certainty and fafety of the method purfued; whereby the perfon foon recovered.

THERE was even a feeming *aquæ pavor;* with fome other fymptoms, which, at firft, made the Phyfician doubt, whether it might not be real Hydrophobia.

THE ftory got abroad, that he had cured a cafe of *rabies canina,* and for fome time it was the current converfation of the neighbourhood. This induced my revered friend, who relates me the cafe, to enquire of the Doctor, with whom he was on terms of intimacy, concerning the truth of the tranfaction. —The Doctor, however, freely confeffed to him, that he believed all the fymptoms might be explained on the principle of fear alone, without having recourfe to Hydrophobia,

phobia, which, it was his real opinion, never exifted.—We know that convulfions, and many other evils, have been induced by fear, and, for years, exercifed fuch force over the patient as to produce much mifery.

It has been generally thought, that thofe affected with this unhappy malady always die mad. This is a miftake. No madnefs attends it. The patients can converfe as rationally as ever, during the time they are ill. This may be proved from almoft every cafe of the difeafe. All authors who have feen it, confirm this, and generally note it down in their relation of the fymptoms.

In the laft day, or fo, of illnefs, delirium, and ravings, for the moft part, come on, with great violence—continue fome time, when they yield, and there is a lucid interval, when the patient difcovers his rationality, anfwering with propriety fuch queftions as are put to him, and fhewing no defire whatever to do mifchief. Thefe paroxifms of

S   deli-

delirium cannot be called madnefs; they bear no relation to what we generally underftand by this term.

From this miftaken notion proceeded that cruel practice of fmothering the unhappy patient between two beds, or ftopping his breath between two pillows.—I hope, for the fake of humanity, it will never again be practifed.—We have pointed out, that the period of the difeafe, at moft, is but fhort—and though we may defpair of curing it—we may, and ought, to adminifter every degree of comfort to the afflicted which can be done.—Should this notion prevail, all will forfake him; and it will then be confidered as expedient to cut fhort his life.—This has, indeed, too often happened.—Van Swieten tells us, " Even " this feverity has been practifed by direct " permiffion from the fuperior magiftrate." —But he very juftly adds,—" 'Tis, however, " cruel to kill a man becaufe we cannot " cure him."—The fame barbarity is alfo repro-

reprobated by Tulpius,*—and ought, in the ftrongeft language to be reprobated by every man who has attended to the nature of the difeafe.

I AM not fure how far even their faliva is dangerous; I fhould, however, be afraid of a bite from a perfon under the difeafe, though I can give no direct proof that it can be communicated by the human race. I read of fome diffections, where the operator fcratched his finger while he infpected the body, and where much more inflammation and pain followed, than is generally found from trifling wounds with an inftrument not infected or befmeared with faliva, or other fluids from the corpfe of an hydrophobic. But this does not reach far enough for

a proof

---

* " Opus non fuit, nec huic, nec aliis ægris (quos
" equedem vidi fatis frequentes) mortem maturare, five
" per ftragula, five per culcitram (uti loquitur vulgus)
" ore impofitam. Pereunt quippe per fe fatis celeriter:
" ut pote raro fuperftites, cum aquæ formidine, in diem
" vel tertium vel quartum."—Vid. Obf. Med. l. 1.
cap. 20. p. 42.

a proof that the difeafe may be communicated in this way.

WITH refpect to the canine tribe, we
find, from the authority of authors, that in-
ftruments ufed in killing mad dogs, and
left unwiped, can, after a long time, like
a lancet infected with variolous matter,
communicate the malady; as alfo threads
wetted with it. We have adduced examples of all thefe in a former part of thefe
pages. Yet it has been known, that perfons have, without injury, put their fingers
into an hydrophobic's mouth, and, unhurt,
drawn out, from time to time, the vifcid,
ropy faliva from thence, that gives fo much
uneafinefs. This was the cafe with the
keeper of Dr. Munckley's patient.* Here
he not only efcaped free from danger, but
had not the leaft apprehenfion from his biting.—Yet all this was done in the very laft
ftage of the difeafe.

WHILE

---

* Vid. Appendix.

WHILE I fay this, however, I do not mean to give a decided opinion on the fubject; neither do I wifh to diffuade perfons from a proper regard to their fafety, who attend fuch patients.—As to the noife, refembling the barking of a dog, which is fo often talked of—it is nothing more than the patient's endeavours to get rid of the vifcid faliva, which is now preternaturally fecreted, and which excites the fame uneafy fenfations as water itfelf.—The voice is indeed changed from its natural tone by the difeafe ; the other is a mere hawking up of fomething irritating, and troublefome in the throat.—A heated imagination may, on fome occafions, call it barking ; but, accurate obfervation, and rational induction, will always draw a very different conclufion.

WE proceed next to a part of our fubject, that, of late, has been the occafion of fome public animadverfions between the author of thefe pages, and an ingenious anonymous writer,

writer; I mean the WORMING OF DOGS.—
Though this be a matter of lefs moment,
yet, having a near connection with canine
madnefs, in as far as it has been, almoft
time out of mind, practifed, it behoves us
to enter a little more minutely into its confideration.

I DOUBT not but it muft have been a
common practice much earlier than the
days of Pliny the Second, though it is
from his writings the commencement is
generally dated. In a great part of his
Natural Hiftory, he only collects together
things he had either read of, or feen; and,
among thefe, it is but natural to conclude,
he had feen the practice of dog-worming,
and that it was common in his days, and,
perhaps, kept up, by cuftom, from a much
earlier date.

HE has been, however, but fhort on the
fubject: but here, as in many other parts
of his work, he has been decifive in his
opi-

opinion, though erroneous.—" Eſt vermi-
" culus in lingua canum, qui vocatur a
" Grecis Lytra, quo exempto infantibus
" catulis, nec rabidi fiant, nec faſtidium
" ſentiunt."*

HERE is the whole paſſage, to which
not only our forefathers, but ourſelves, have
paid, even almoſt to the end of the eigh-
teenth century, and in the face of phyſio-
logy, and improved philoſophy, implicit
obedience, and given to it a ſtupid belief.

SOME few, however, muſt be exempted
from this charge of ſimple credulity, who
have ventured to aſſert its inſignificancy.—
Among theſe, Dr. James is firſt to be
reckoned. The Doctor was a profeſſed
Dog Doctor, and was conſulted on the ſub-
ject from all parts of England, by ſportſ-
men, and others who bred this animal. He
ſpoke, no doubt, from experience: he muſt
have

---

* Vid. Plin. Nat. Hiſt. lib. 29. c. 5.

have feen many run mad who had been
wormed, and bite likewife; yet he has
omitted to give us any examples; and
hence, what he has faid has generally been
looked on as a matter of opinion, and little
regard paid to it.—Dr. Berkenhaut, lately,
in fome obfervations on the fubject, has
alfo treated it with the contempt it deferves.
—And, on weighing the fubject, in like
manner, I could not avoid feeing its abfurdity, and being fully of their opinion.

I SHALL quote what Dr. James fays on
the fubject. About to reprobate feveral
prophylactics, the Doctor fays,—" The firft
" I fhall endeavour to fet a mark of infamy
" upon, is that operation which is called
" *worming a dog*; and the rather, becaufe
" the notion many people have, that no
" dog can go mad after it; and of others,
" who firmly believe, that a dog thus
" treated cannot bite, though he fhould be
" afterwards mad, may have very untoward
" confequences, by lulling thofe of this
" opi-

" opinion into a fatal fecurity, whilft they
" are converfant with the domeftic animals
" that have fuffered this ridiculous cruelty.

" I HAVE frequently feen dogs wormed,
" as they call it, and find it thus : there is
" in almoft every town, or village, in Eng-
" land; fome cobler, or farrier, or huntf-
" man, that boafts a dexterity in taking a
" worm from under the tongue of a puppy.
" Their fee is ufually from a fhilling, for
" dogs of the more genteel fort, to a
" penny, or a mug of ale, for curs.—They
" elevate the tongue, and with an awl, or
" a pen-knife, or fome pointed inftrument,
" make a puncture under it, and draw out
" a very flender filament, which I take to
" be a *nerve*; and this contracting when
" recently taken away, the idiots fancy it
" ftirs, and believe it a worm, to which it
" bears no manner of refemblance.

" BE that as it may, I am *certain* from
" *experience*, that dogs thus treated, run

T   " mad

" mad equally with thofe who have never
" fuffered this abfurd operation. There is
" no worm in the part, I firmly believe,
" and, confequently, none can be taken out.
" All that this can do is, to prevent puppies
" from biting or knawing every thing they
" meet with; and for no other reafon, than
" becaufe it makes their mouths fore, and
" gives them pain when they take any hard
" thing in their mouths; and this breaks
" them of the habit."*

HERE, however, it is to be obferved, the
Doctor is miftaken when he calls it a nerve.
More accurate obfervation would have taught
him, that it wanted even fimilitude to a nerve.
Nerves are foft and pulpy fubftances, and do
not contract on being cut. On the contrary,
they elongate themfelves a little. This,
without going farther, ought to have pointed
out the improbability of this organ's being
a nerve. To deny its being a worm, is altogether fuperfluous; I believe, the moft
ftre-

---

* Vid. Dr. James on Canine Madnefs.

ftrenuous advocates for *worming* have given up this idea.

DR. BRODIE differs from others in his opinion of it. He thinks it is a gland. On this fuppofition he has imagined, that there may be truth in the common notion, that wormed dogs do not run mad; or, if they fhould go mad, as obfervation proves has been the cafe, as much as if they had not been deprived of it, they are thereby rendered incapable, it is thought, of communicating the difeafe.

THOSE who fupport the idea of its being a gland, argue, that it is neceffary for the feparation of the poifon at the mouth; and hence this gland is given to the animal. Therefore, if it be extracted, the poifon cannot be communicated, becaufe the organ neceffary to make the feparation does now no longer exift.

THIS,

THIS, no doubt, would have been found reasoning, had the foundation been firm. But this happens not to be the case; the thing itself is not true. It is no gland. This part of the argument should have first been well examined; and then there would have been more certainty of the security of the building; which, unluckily, for want of this precaution, tumbles at once in a ruinous heap.

IN the first place, it is not like any other gland in the body. No duct has yet been discovered going out from it, by which, like all other glands the excreted liquor is to be carried away. The parotids, the sublinguals, and all other conglomerate glands, have a canal running from them to the place where the contents are to make their exit, or be deposited, for the purposes of nature.

THE

The conglobate, or lymphatic glands, as they are more generally called, have their respective lymphatic veffels, or ducts, to carry the contents to the great receptacle, or thoracic duct, which pours its contents again into the blood. It becomes, indeed, the very effence of a gland to have a duct; but no fuch thing has been difcovered here. This alone might convince us, it was no more a gland, than a worm.

Morgagni, who has taken fome pains to inveftigate its nature, and whofe opinion in what refpects anatomical refearches, the public place juft confidence in, on moft occafions, tells us, it is compofed of liga-ment and tendon; and gives it the term of tendinous-ligament.* Had he found reafon to fuppofe it a gland, he would have told us on what grounds he had founded his opinion.

But

---

* De Cauf. & Sedib. Morbor. l. 1. eff. 8. art. 35.

But the naked eye can most distinctly and evidently trace these two substances, separately, of which this eminent anatomist tells us it is composed, in a longitudinal direction, and parallel to each other. The one appears clear, and semi-transparent; the other, dark in its colour. The tendon ends with the body or bulky part; the ligament grows smaller, and leaving the tendon behind, runs out alone, in length near an inch, in one now in my possession, and small, like a fine thread, or rather hair, to connect itself with the substance of the tongue towards its root. What may be the real use of this little organ in dogs, I must leave to more able and accurate physiologists to determine; but, that it is for a different purpose than what many attribute to it, appears to me not only probable, but a rational conclusion.

Some, who have given up the idea of its extraction on the grounds of preventing

dogs

dogs from going mad, have yet maintained, that fuch dogs. though they might go mad, never attempted either to bite, or to run away, but died fullen, or fleepy mad, as they exprefs it. This is the opinion of the gentleman who wrote fome remarks on the fubject, addreffed to me.* He thinks wormed dogs cannot bite when mad :— " Experience having fhewn," he fays, " time out of mind, that by taking " out the tendon that grows under the " tongue, not one fingle inftance has ever " happened of any perfon being bit by a " dog fo wormed. And it has been ob- " ferved," he goes on, ". that out of feveral " packs of hounds, and many other dogs, " that have been mad, thofe wormed have " fallen off their meat, refufed water, and " always died fullen, or fleepy mad, not " one of them ever offering to bite any " thing; when other dogs, part of the fame " pack of hounds, which were neglected " to be wormed, though bit at the fame

time

---

* Vid. Ipfwich Journal for Feb. 1785.

" time by the fame mad dog, have acted as
" ufual, biting every thing that came in
" their way."—The account here given
feems to have been taken from fome huntf-
man, incapable of diftinguifhing phænomena, or one difeafe from another: for he
does not give it as his own; though he
builds reafoning on it; as appears from his
faying, " It has been obferved," &c.*

I was aware, that his eafinefs of belief,
and confidence in the accuracy of others,
led him to produce thefe as proofs in favour
of worming, though reafon ftarted up in
oppofition to them. Truth, however, not
the love of victory alone (for which, independent of truth, no man fhould ever con-
tend in philofophic inveftigations) led me
to enquire farther into the fubject; when
I was fortunate enough to procure examples
fufficient to eftablifh my firft opinion, and
to leave no pretence hereafter for the practice of dog-worming.

It

---

* Vid. appendix for the difpute at large.

IT fhould, however, be remembered, that madnefs is not the only diftemper to which dogs are liable. Many have, no doubt, been called mad, that were affected with other difeafes.—Dr. James, whofe authority in thefe cafes has, indeed, much weight, fays there are two forts of madnefs; one which he calls *raving madnefs*; and is attended with delirium: the other, *dumb madnefs*, accompanied with a fort of *coma*. Thefe are the terms, he fays, ufed by the huntfmen. In the laft, the dog lies ftupid, and, as it were, fenfelefs, " taking no man-" ner of notice of any body, or any thing, " till he dies, never attempting to bite."* According to the gentleman quoted above, thefe would have all been wormed dogs. But had they been fo, Dr. James would not have omitted to mention it. For then it would have been a fufficient, and cogent reafon for his recommending worming;

U   whereas

---

* Vid. Dr. James on Canine Madnefs.

whereas, he takes pains, as we have already feen, to reprobate its abfurdity.—It would appear, that this laft is a fort of fever incident to the animal, and materially different from the other, which is termed *rabies*.

THERE is an evident difproportion between the caufe, and the effect which is faid to be produced, in attributing to the extraction of the little fubftance already taken notice of, to the prevention either of madnefs, or of the animal's incapability of biting when rabid. This cannot fail at once to ftrike an unprejudiced mind. I wifhed ardently to put the matter to the iffue of pofitive proof by experiment, the firft opportunity, as it appeared to me to carry with it a glaring inconfiftency.

MR. RIPSHAW, keeper of Ipfwich gaol, however, afforded me ample fatisfaction on this head, fooner than I expected.— He had read in the Ipfwich Journal what had been faid on the fubject, both for and
againft

againſt it.—He has himſelf wormed many hundreds of dogs; and is a conſiderable Dog Doctor.—He has often alſo diſſected this animal: therefore, his teſtimony in a caſe of this kind, as his veracity cannot be diſputed, muſt appear deciſive.

He relates, and is ready to atteſt, when called on, that, among others, he wormed a dog for one Cutting, a butcher in this town (Ipſwich). That the dog not only went mad, but bit a cow, a gander, and a ſpaniel of his own, on which he ſet great value. The cow and the gander went, ſoon after, mad; and, to prevent the ſame event in his own dog, he ſhot him; and adds, that the loſs gave him great uneaſineſs.

At another time, two other dogs he had wormed alſo went mad, and both ran away —(the dog we have already mentioned like-wiſe ran away)—but he cannot aſſert whe-ther they bit other animals.—He wormed alſo another, when it was a puppy of about

four

four months old. It remained well till about three years after, *i. e.* till about half a year ago; when it went mad, ran away from its mafter, and bit a great number of other dogs, feveral of whom went mad foon after. All this can be attefted by different people in this place, fo that the facts are eftablifhed on the fureft foundation of accurate obfervation, and faithful relation.

THUS far of worming.—Though, for the moft part, the difeafe is communicated by the bite of an infected animal, yet it may not always proceed from this fource. Peculiar circumftances may generate it, independent of a bite. Long continued heat; and, authors fay, alfo long continued cold, may predifpofe, in a certain meafure, to its production: if to this be added putrid flefh meat, want of water, and of proper exercife; thefe will be other powerful concomitant caufes. It is likewife to be confidered, that the dog is a fpecies of animal that nature has not endowed with perfpirable pores; hence no

per-

perfpirable matter can pafs off from the
body, as in other animals, the whole paffing off by the lungs alone. This may, in
like manner, contribute its fhare towards
rendering the fluids more acrid, and become
an additional occafional caufe, while the
whole uniting, may produce a *fever fui ge-
neris*, and beget a *poifon* dreadful in its confequences to every fpecies of animals that
receive it into their fyftem.

THE maftiffs which we keep to watch
our houfes, and which are, perhaps, the
moft ufeful fpecies of this domeftic animal,
are, for the moft part, confined to the treatment mentioned here. Their food confifts
chiefly of putrid horfe-flefh, and offals of the
animals killed for our own fuftenance. It is
by this means we give them that fiercenefs
and boldnefs for which they are valued. This
is often kept fo long after we purchafe it
for them, that it becomes almoft a mafs of
corruption itfelf before it be finifhed. We
may judge what changes it is then capable
of

of making on the fluids. We, for the moſt part, chain them up. Hence it is impoſſible they can get ſufficient exerciſe, without which no animal can be healthy. Servants are but too often negligent in what is required of them as their duty, and ſhould the taſk of giving them water be entirely left to their care, there is but too much reaſon to ſuppoſe they will be but very indifferently ſupplied. As they are chained up all day, they cannot relieve themſelves. It would be well, if better attention were paid to theſe circumſtances.

BOERHAAVE is wrong when he tells us, dogs in the firſt ſtage of madneſs refuſe all meat and drink. The caſes we quote prove the contrary. And this ought to be the more attended to, as it is a common, though very erroneous notion, almoſt univerſally received by all ranks. But, as it is fraught with danger, I think it incumbent on me to warn the public of the fatal ſecurity that may proceed from it.
Many

Many cafes might be quoted to prove the fallacy of this opinion. Dogs fo infected as to produce the difeafe, as experience on too many occafions has pointed out, will fawn on their mafter or others, fly up and lick their hands in good nature, will take food when offered, without any perceptible change, and appear nearly as in health, only their temper is fomewhat more eafily ruffled. This, however, conftitutes an early ftage of the difeafe. And now, in cafes of any fufpicion, they fhould conftantly be tied up.

It is a bad method to kill a fufpected dog : for then it is not eafy to afcertain the fact; and fhould it fo happen, that perfons are bit by him, it leaves them ever after under the dread of apprehenfion.

In the Academy of Sciences we are furnifhed with an experiment to prove whether a dog was really mad, who may thus prematurely be killed. How far it is a teft
I dare

I dare not fay. We are directed there to rub a piece of boiled meat on the teeth and gums of the animal killed on fufpicion; and then offer it to another dog. If he was affected with madnefs, we are affured, the dog to which this piece is offered, will fly from it with fear and horror, barking and howling : if not mad, he will devour it inftantly.*

If this teft be found good, it cannot fail to prove very ufeful; efpecially as many a dog is hunted down, and falls a martyr to the blind zeal of the injudicious populace, and the hue and cry raifed by ignorance and precipitate outrage.

A FAR

---

* Sir Thomas Myern directs, that the feathers may be plucked from the breaft of an old cock, and applied bare to the bite. This is to be done on every wound given. If the dog was mad, we are told, the cock will fwell and die, and the perfon bit, do well; but, if the cock dies not, the dog was not mad.—A moft accurate and effectual method, truly, of diftinguifhing *rabies* in this animal !—But it accords with the fuperftition and ignorance of the times.

A FAR different treatment fhould, on fufpicion of madnefs, be followed. If the animal be killed, the truth can never be afcertained; and fhould perfons be bit by him, their apprehenfions muft continue; whereby they muft feel all the horrors of their fuppofed dangerous fituation, and all the anxiety that doubt can create.

BUT, fhould he be inftantly tied up, till time had afcertained his real ftate, either their fears would be removed, or the danger they ftood in demonftrated, whereby they might have it in their power to ufe fuch precautions as may be judged moft proper and expedient in thefe circumftances.

IT has already been taken notice of, how feldom perfons become affected with hydrophobia, even though bit by animals really rabid. We may fay, that, on an average, perhaps, not one out of twelve to fixteen, ever fuffer any injury.—Mr. Hunter knew

X   where

where no lefs than twenty-one were bit
by a mad dog, and only one of them took
the difeafe. Dr. Vaughan tells us, that
only one, whofe cafe he relates, took it,
though between twenty and thirty were bit
by the fame dog. Many other obfervations
tend to confirm it. This, furely, is the
kind interpofition of the Diety in our favour, that a difeafe fo deftructive, and, as
yet, beyond human fagacity to remove,
fhould fo feldom occur, in proportion to
the numbers that receive injury from infected animals.

And here arifes another queftion, worthy,
perhaps, of being afcertained, i. e. whether
as Dr. James will have it, dogs fly from
perfons actually infected ? If fo, it would
appear to be a ftrong proof of the falutary
inftinct of the canine tribe. They fhun
one another when infected; the acutenefs
of their olfactory organs, it would feem,
gives them notice of fome baneful change
in the fluids, by the difagreeable effluvia
which

which now taints the air, and is offensive to them.

MAY not the fame be reasonably suppofed of their fagacity, and acuteness of fmell, with respect to the human race? There appears nothing unnatural in the suppofition; nor is the analogy, by any means, diftant.

SEVERAL authors who have wrote on this difeafe, have talked much about the new and full moon; and the effects of their medicines when given at thefe times, in preference to any other; and alfo, that thefe were the moft likely times for Hydrophobia to fhew itfelf.—No regard is to be paid to this.

WHEN Mr. George Dampier recommended his Jew's-ear [vid. Philof. Tranf. No. 237] on which Dr. Mead afterwards, placed fo high a value, under the name of *Pulvis Antyliffus,* he tells us, that after a

dog

dog hath bitten man or beaſt, the effects do
not begin to appear till after the new, and
full moon. This, in part, however, is true;
but true in a different ſenſe, from that in
which it was then generally underſtood.
We have both new and full moon in the
ſpace of a month; and we know, the dif-
eaſe ſeldom makes its appearance ſooner.—
Hence, in this ſenſe, it may be true; and
now the obſervation becomes a farther
proof of what has been already pointed
out, that few caſes of the diſeaſe appear at
an earlier period after the bite:—but, in
the other ſenſe, it is advanced on ſuper-
ficial obſervation; is fabulous; and without foundation in truth.

ANOTHER period, beſides the new and
full moon, has been held, by ſome, as more
than commonly ominous; this is the aniverſary of the unhappy accident. Perſons
who have been bit, have had their appre-
henſions kept alive, and encreaſed about
this time.—They thought, that if the diſeaſe

eafe was to appear, it would begin its at-
tacks on this day, in preference to any
other.—This is a vulgar error; yet it has
caufed much uneafinefs, not only to thofe
who come more immediately under this
denomination, but to perfons of no mean
underftandings.

WE have touched already on the effects
of imagination, and the power it has in
producing difeafe. A proof of its powers,
as well as of this error, may be given from
a popular publication, now almoft in every
one's hands.—Mrs. Belamy tells us, fhe
fuffered much from this:—" I had" fays
fhe, " difcharged my lodgings in town,
" (London) together with my footman and
" maid-fervant; I had fent my Black to
" Mr. Woodward, and kept only my old
" Grace, a blackbird, and a favourite *dog*.

" THE latter had for fome days appeared
" to be ill, and refufed all food; when,
" upon calling him, in order to induce
" him

" him to eat, the little animal flew to me,
" with feeming fondnefs, and fixed his
" teeth in my upper lip. Mr. Woodward,
" who happened to be prefent, inftantly ex-
" claimed,—" I hope you do not bleed !"—
" This, with my obferving affectionate ap-
" prehenfions in the looks of every perfon
" in the room, made me conclude the dog
" to be mad, and that I fhould partake
" of this malady.—I was confequently fei-
" zed with inexpreffible horrors ;—and, if
" I did not fear death itfelf, yet I could not
" help being fhocked when I imagined him
" (Death) to be approaching with unufual
" terrors.

" IT is well known," fhe goes on, " that
" dangers appear much more alarming in
" apprehenfion than in reality. My feel-
" ings, on this prefent occafion, confirmed
" this truth ; for Mr. Bromfield, who had
" been fent for as foon as the accident hap-
" pened, declared, that I felt infinitely more
" than if the falival infection had operated
" in

" in its full force. Such a deep impreſſion
" did this event make on my mind, that,
" for ſeveral years after, I was in *agonies*,
" upon the *aniverſary* of the day on which
" it happened." *

It will be to me infinite ſatisfaction, if
I can become the means of removing, from
the minds of any of my fellow-creatures,
the dread occaſioned by a belief in theſe
erroneous and hurtful notions.

I wish, for the ſafety of individuals, we
bred fewer of theſe animals than is now in
faſhion. We ſeem to be multiplying the
breed without end—and this alſo without
any good whatever in view. We throw
away on our dogs what might be of great
ſervice to the poor—in this, I cannot help
thinking, we are criminal. A tax on dogs,
I am ſincerely of opinion, would prove of
public utility, as well in regard to the prevention

---

* Apology, Vol. IV. p. 137.

vention of Hydrophobia, as in a political view.—With politics, however, I have no bufinefs.—But, furely, the accidents happening from thefe animals becoming rabid, muft bear fome proportion to their numbers.

I SHALL now, to fave my readers fome trouble in turning over the works of au‐ thors, colleƐt the principal parts of the praƐtice followed in a few cafes of the malady. I fhall begin with Dr. Fothergill's patient—Mr. Charles Belamy of Holborn.

AFTER giving us the fymptoms, with an account how the accident of the bite took place, the DoƐtor fays, " To gain a " little time for refleƐtion, on a cafe fo fud‐ " den and fo dangerous, and that nothing " which feemed reafonable to be done, " might in the mean time be omitted, I "ordered fix ounces of blood to be taken " from the arm ; that a fcruple of native " cinnabar, and half a fcruple of mufk, " made into a bolus, might be given every
" four

" four hours; and that as much nourish-
" ment, fruit, or any thing he chose, might
" be got down, as possible."—Dr. Watson
was called in to the Doctor's assistance—
they met at five the same evening.—He
had taken only two of the boluses, a few
bits of bread moistened with wine, some
strawberries, a few bits of pudding, but had
not attempted to drink any liquor. They
begged him to drink some liquid for their
satisfaction :—he consented.—" He threw
" it hastily into his mouth, and swallowed
" it with difficulty, and extreme pertur-
" bation. The moment the liquor touched
" the *gula,* all the muscles concerned in
" deglutition appeared to be convulsed."—
No evacuation by stool to-day.—" Upon
" maturely considering this very hazardous
" state of things, we agreed on the follow-
" ing process :"—" That he should then be
" carried to the warm bath, and remain in
" it, so long, and to such a degree of heat,
" as was most agreeable to himself. Next
" a glister of a pint of milk and water to be

" adminiftered : This to be repeated as of-
" ten as it could be conveniently done. In
" the laft of thefe clyfters a dram of Dover's
" powder was to be given."

" THAT two drams of ftrong mercurial
" ointment fhould be rubbed by himfelf on
" his legs and thighs, as foon as he returned
" from the bath, and that he fhould endea-
" vour to get down all the fuftenance he
" could." Next day, the report received,
was, " the laxative clyfter had produced a
" proper effect. The warm bath relieved
" him greatly whilft he was in it, fo that
" for a time, as he expreffed it, his fufferings
" were fufpended." Slept none all night—
great diftrefs—copious flow of faliva—
pulfe hard and quick.—They agreed, " that
" he fhould be blooded ftanding, according
" as his ftrength would bear ; that he fhould
" be conveyed to the warm bath, and re-
" main as long as he could, agreeable to
" himfelf, that as foon as he returned from
" it, the clyfter, with a dram of Dover's
powder

" powder, fhould be adminiftered ; and that
" half an ounce of mercurial ointment
" fhould be rubbed on his legs and thighs as
" foon after as might be done conveniently ;
" and alfo on coming out of the bath, three
" grains of Theb. Extr. to be given ; and
" two every hour after." This vifit was in
the morning.—At five this evening alfo
they again vifited : he received them with
the utmoft tranfports of joy ; and " de-
" fcribed in very ftrong terms the pleafure,
" and the benefit he received from the warm
" bath, and the hopes he now conceived of
" a fpeedy recovery. He had not flept a
" moment from the time he was feized with
" the dread of liquors. He repeatedly ex-
" preffed the fatisfaction he received from
" the bath, and wifhed to go into it again.
" They confented." This was the third
time ; but he now felt himfelf confiderably more agitated at the fight of the water—his refolution almoft forfook him—
putting in, on much intreaty, one foot—
then haftily withdrawing it, &c.—at length

he

he went in, and remained in it half an hour. He died two hours after.

Dr. Vaughan's patient, a boy of eight years of age. The accident happened in 1778.

THE Doctor tells us, he began with the warm bath—" the fight of which occafi-
" oned fome commotion, and produced
" marks of difguft and fear. Thefe were
" overcome by perfuafion, and he was pla-
" ced in it. The moment he touched the
" water, his painful fobbing and difguft to
" it were encreafed. Thefe fubfided in a
" few feconds, and he then told me he felt
" eafier; but it was obfervable, that thefe
" fymptoms were renewed as oft as a frefh
" furface was touched by the water. He
" was kept in the bath near three-quarters
" of an hour, during which time he fre-
" quently faid, that he felt lefs annoyance
" from his diforder."

ON

On coming out of the water, a plaifter was applied to his throat, of which Sachar. Saturn. was the bafis. The Doctor now tried what could be done by the metalline antifpafmodics, and he prefcribed the fol- lowing :

R. Flor. Zinc. gr. j.
    Cupr. Ammon. Semigran.
    Mofch. opt. gr. x.
Syr. Simpl. Q.S. ut fiant pilulæ duæ mol- les; Sumantur hor. tert. vel quart. quoque.

A liniment, confifting of three drams of the ftrong mercurial ointment, with the fame quantity of oil of amber, was to be rubbed on the fhoulders and back; and a clyfter, made of five ounces of frefh broth, with thirty drops of laudanum, was to be injected foon after going to bed. To thefe the Doctor added a medical atmofphere, made by burning G. Ammon. in his room.

Between

" BETWEEN nine and ten o'clock this evening, he took fome bits of bread foaked in milk, but with difficulty."

AT eleven o'clock the pills were repeated. At twelve the fymptoms encreafed greatly. He was again put into the warm bath; and after coming out, a broth clyfter, with a dram of Tinct. Theb. was ordered to be in-jected; and the mercurial liniment to be repeated. He continued now near two hours in the warm bath, " feeling himfelf much " more comfortable the whole time." Both the clyfters he had got come away, bringing with them fome hardened feces.

EACH dofe of his pills were now ordered to contain two grains of Cupr. Ammon. the fame quantity of Theb. Extr. three grains of Fl. Zinc. with ten grains of Aff. Fœtid. which was fubftituted for the mufk; whilft a folution of that Fœtid Gum, with a dram of Tinct. Theb. was adminiftered as a clyfter.

ter. The above pills, though repeated every four hours, afforded not the fmalleft relief; " nor did they fhew the leaft action upon " the frame."

At eight o'clock in the morning he ex- preffed a ftrong defire of going into the warm bath again. " This was complied with; a " temperate one of *milk* and *water* being " fpeedily prepared. He went into it; but " with perturbation—though temperate, yet " he complained greatly of its heat: in a " quarter of an hour he was weary, and de- " fired to be taken out of it. A purgative " clyfter was afterwards given to remove " fome little fullnefs that was in the " bowels."

" Seeing of how little avail every thing " had hitherto proved, and being clearly " convinced of his inevitable fate," fays the Doctor, " I was at length determined to put " in force the remedy which Helmont " fpeaks of in terms fo favourable; but let

me

" me add, not with much expectation that
" this would prove more fuccefsful than
" thofe powerful ones, which hitherto in
" every cafe had been fo fruitlefsly em-
" ployed."

A large tub of cold water, well faturated
with common falt, was made ready, into
which this patient was fuddenly plunged
over head and ears, and there held until he
ceafed to ftruggle. He was then taken out,
and the fame operation again repeated, until
he became fo quiet, that it was apprehended
a total extinction of life would actually
have taken place.

He was then wrapt in a blanket, and put
to bed, where he remained more quiet than
he had been any part of the preceding night,
and fo continued for near two hours. He
now repeated his medicine; all his bad
fymptoms returned with added force. At
eight o'clock he took fome pills of camphire

and

and nitre, with two grains of opium. He died a little before two.

A second patient treated by Dr. Vaughan.
*—He was twenty-five years of age, and
the accident happened in 1775.*

THE warm bath was ufed as in the other; alfo the purgative clyfter: this procured a ftool.—A fecond was to be thrown up, confifting of four ounces of oil, with half an ounce of Extr. Theb.—Four grains of Ung. Cærul. Fort. were to be rubbed on the fauces, and the part to be covered afterwards with the cataplafm. e Cymino; to which was added half an ounce of Extr. Theb.

AN embrocation was applied to the region of the ftomach, with continued friction, confifting of Sp. Sal. Ammon. half an ounce—Ol. Olivar. ten drams; fix drams of oil of amber; and ten drams of laudanum.

Z   STRONG

STRONG mercurial ointment, to the amount of two ounces, to be rubbed on the back and shoulders; and, as a farther means to induce a speedy salivation, he was to receive the smoke of cinnabar into the mouth, by throwing a dram of that substance now and then upon a hot iron—thus of external means. The internal were as follows :—R. Mosch. opt. gr. xv.—Mercur. Emet. flav. gr. iij.—Extr. Theb. gr. iv.— Syr. Simp. q. s. f. Bol. Mollis.

WHILE in the warm bath, he felt himself easier also—under the application of the ointment—but the plan did not succeed— he died.

A third patient treated by Dr. Vaughan.

AFTER the Doctor relates the symptoms, which are not to be repeated here, he tells us, " In this situation he (the patient) was

" or-

" ordered to go to bed; having firſt ſwal-
" lowed a ſcruple of muſk, with two grains
" of Extr. Theb. made into a ſoft bolus."—
He was fourteen years of age—his name,
Thomas Nourſe.

AFTER reflecting on the nature of the
diſeaſe (it is to be obſerved, this was the
firſt of his three patients) he gave a compoſition of fifteen grains of muſk; one of
Turbeth mineral; and five grains of Extr.
Theb. made into a ſoft bolus; and this
to be repeated every three hours:—an
ounce of ſtrong mercurial ointment was
likewiſe directed to be rubbed on the
cervical vertebræ, and ſhoulders; and the
following embrocation ordered to be applied to the throat, renewing it as often
as the part grew dry:—R. Tinct. Theb.
unc. du.—Acet. Saturn. ſemiunc. M.
—He could not bear this to touch him
without being thrown into convulſions;
therefore, the following was ſubſtituted,
which he bore very well:—R. Extr. Theb.
ſemi-

femiunc.—Camphor. fp. vin. in pulv. redact.
drachm. tref.—Confect. Damocrat. drachm.
fex—M. f. Empl. faucibus externis ap-
plicandum.—The warm bath was kept in
readinefs, but he could not bear the touch
of water.—Before he came under the Doctor's care, he had taken the celebrated Ormfkirk medicine, and had bathed in the fea:
this procefs was entered on the day after he
was bit.—He was bled on the Tuefday
morning, and took another dofe of the
Ormfkirk, which was the day the Doctor
firft faw him.—At two o'clock he repeated
the mufk medicines mentioned above, with
lefs hefitation than he had done before;
and, " was more comfortable to himfelf,
" and, with tolerable eafe, got down fome
" mouthfuls of bread and butter."—His
medicines were again repeated at five; and
he took them with as little difficulty as the
laft—" Matters, therefore," fays the Doctor, " wearing a lefs terrible afpect, I could
" not help flattering myfelf with hopes, that
" this dreadful diforder would at length be
" con-

" conquered by the combined powers of
" mufk, opium, and mercury.—My expec-
" tation was of fhort continuance." For
in two hours after, it feems, every fymptom
recurred with greater violence.

At eight o'clock in the evening his medicines were again repeated :—he took them
now with reluctance.—An hour after, every
thing wore a worfe appearance.—He took
five grains of opium without mufk—and
Turbeth mineral; but with great difficulty.
—Another ounce of mercurial ointment
was rubbed on his fhoulders; and half an
ounce of Tinct. Theb. mixed with fix
ounces of mutton broth, was given by way
of clyfter.—The difeafe ftill encreafed—at
eleven o'clock, every thing was worfe.—In
the next paragraph the Doctor gives us a
melancholy picture :—" He had alfo all his
" complaints aggravated by the improper
" conduct of his attendants; who, prompted
" by their fears, had almoft perfuaded them-
" felves, that the opinion univerfally re-
" ceived

" ceived by the common people, of *fmo-*
" *thering* fuch unfortunate objects was not
" only juftifiable but expedient. For I
" found them confining the poor creature
" under the bed-clothes, by the united force
" of half a dozen ftrong affiftants; whofe
" countenances befpoke the terrible appre-
" henfions they were under." The Doctor's humanity immediately fet him at li-
berty.—" Being fenfible of the ill treatment
" he had received, he became fufpicious of
" his attendants, and lefs attentive to my
" inftructions."—Dr. Vaughan feverely re-
primanded them for the treatment they
ufed, and, at the fame time, foothed the
patient, ufing mild perfuafion, by which
means he had his inftructions again obeyed.
—" I had fcarce" fays the Doctor, " left
" the room, before a loud fcream befpoke
" fome unexpected change. Upon turning
" my head to difcover what this meant, the
" boy was at my fhoulders, having fud-
" denly quitted his bed with an intention
" to follow me. To this he immediately
" re-

" returned at my requeſt, without having
" ſhewn the leaſt inclination to bite, or be-
" traying any thing farther than an ill opi-
" nion of thoſe by whom he had been ſo
" improperly treated."—A larger doſe of
opium was given to him—it proved inſfec-
tual.—His ſtrength failed him from this
till about two in the morning—when he
died.

*Mr. Bathie's patient, James Patton,
about fourteen years of age.—The accident happened in November, 1774.*

I SHALL relate how it took place, as the
truth of an aſſertion I have made in theſe
pages will thence appear.

PATTON was a ſhepherd boy; and " in
" the field, in company with two of his fel-
" low-ſervants, who obſerved a ſmall ſheep-
" dog make up to the unfortunate lad, uſing
" the *ordinary demonſtrations* of *tameneſs* and
" *affection* peculiar to that ſpecies of animal
" in

" in a ſtate of health. Far from exhibiting
" any appearance of madneſs, he deceived
" the boy by *fawning upon him*, and, *with-*
" *out reluctance, eat bread,* which he threw
" down to him. One of the men deſired
" the lad to tie a cord about the dog's neck,
" to ſecure him from running away, whilſt
" the other, ſuſpicious of hazard, by ob-
" ſerving his *eye* very much *inflamed* and *dull,*
" called out to the boy to let him alone;
" but he was not attentive to this caution,
" and attempted to faſten the cord round
" the neck of the dog, in which act the
" dog turned and bit the back of his right
" hand, between the ſmall and ring fin-
" gers." He ran off, we are told, and, four
or five days after, was killed as a mad dog
in a different pariſh, by people who had not
heard of this accident.

I THOUGHT it neceſſary to give this part
of the hiſtory of the accident, becauſe it is
generally believed, that if a dog either
fawns, or eats, he cannot be mad :—but
this

this is a moſt dangerous tenent; and, I doubt
not, is the means of lulling to a fatal ſecurity, till the time for prevention of the
evil conſequences has elapſed.*

A a   HE

---

* An accident happened to two perſons in this
neighbourhood, one on the 7th, the other on the 9th
of April laſt: one a boy of about fifteen, the other
about forty.—It was not without conſiderable difficulty I could perſuade ſome gentlemen who then con-
verſed with me on the ſubjeĉt, that the dog was mad,
becauſe he " *eat his food, &c.*" I knew, from the experience of authors, the fallaciouſneſs of this opinion,
and thought it my duty to oppoſe it.—The dog had
been bit ſome weeks before by a mad dog—he was tied
up on ſuſpicion—and had only been a few days libe-
rated when he bit the above people. I requeſted
he might be again tied up, if he returned (for he went
off immediately, and, they added, without his dinner,
which he had never done before). He returned the
ſame night. He was again tied up—this was on Friday.—By Sunday evening he became ſo furious, that
he was declared mad by all who ſaw him, and they became ſo alarmed leſt he might get looſe, that they
knocked him on the head.—When he was firſt tied up,
he bore the chain very well ; but it was very different
now.—So great was his fury, that he wounded his
mouth conſiderably in biting at the chain which held
him, and deeply impreſſed the marks of his teeth in it,
toſſing and raging about at the ſame time. It was
twenty-

THE lad had been three days under Hydrophobia before Mr. Bathie faw him.—His pulfe at this time was from one hundred and twenty-five to one hundred and thirty.—A pound of blood was immediately taken away—nothing remarkable in its appearance.—The difeafe had now got to a great height, and no hopes of a cure. To fatisfy the patient's friends, however, Mr. B. gave him a grain of T. Emet.—he had a propenfity to vomit—Mr. B. thought this might affift it a little. A clyfter had been

or-

_____

twenty-four hours after the lad was bit, before I faw him; and about two from the time the man received his bite. I had the wounds treated as I have directed in this differtation by an ingenious furgeon at Woodbridge (Mr. Page) leaving directions to keep the wounds open as long as it might be thought neceffary; by which means, I hope, they will experience no other inconvenience than what may arife from the keeping a fore open.—But, fhould it turn out otherwife, I fhall think it incumbent on me to lay the whole before the public.—Two fwine were likewife bit at the time with thefe perfons—thefe were alfo ordered to be tied up, to fee what the refult might turn out.—It is now feven weeks fince, and all is yet well.

ordered, but it was not given.—He died about eight in the evening.—The following is worth mentioning :—" When an uncle " of his was offering him a bit of bread, a " little before he grew quiet, *i. e.* a little " before he expired, he made a fnatch, and " bit his thumb; but the man luckily " had the prudence and refolution to cut " out the part that was bit, and fo remains " free from any apprehenfion of hazard."

Treatment of Mr. Babington's patient, Abraham Palmer.—The accident happened on the 9th of June, 1783.

NEITHER excifion nor cauftic was had recourfe to.—" As there was no particular rea- " fon for fuppofing that the dog was mad, " and as excifion, or the application of the " cauftic, would have been painful, if not " dangerous, and perhaps with difficulty " fubmitted to, it was judged fufficient to " direct, that the hand fhould be well fo- " mented with milk and water, to get it foft

and

" and clean, and that about a dram of ftrong
" *mercurial ointment* fhould be rubbed in
" every day for four or five days, dreffing
" the wounds afterwards fuperficially, with
" a little lint and cerate." It is worthy of
remark here, that " there was no *particular*
" *reafon* for fuppofing that the dog was
" mad."—Hence the prudent fufpicion that
fhould be entertained on receiving a bite
from any dog—and the neceffity of fpeedy
action accordingly:—to truft to chance, is
fporting with life. Nothing more was
heard of the boy (he was about fourteen
years of age) till Thurfday the 17th of
July, when he returned to Mr. Babington.
He had felt fome fymptoms the day before
—the cafe was evident.—" The period was
" now paft when any advantage could be
" expected from local applications, yet hu-
" manity required that fomething fhould
" be attempted."—He was ordered the
Tonquin medicine, or fomething like it,
viz. every two hours he was to take a bolus, confifting of mufk and factitious cinnabar,

nabar, each fifteen grains—and one grain of opium. At eight o'clock this evening (Thurfday) he had no unufual fecretion of faliva—but he could not bear water. At nine the mufk was encreafed to a fcruple.— The cinnabar and opium were given in the fame dofes as before. A clyfter was di-rected—it had no effect. He fuffered his hands and feet to be put into warm water— yet with great reluctance.—" At one o'clock " (Friday) his countenance and manner " were ftrongly marked with *horror* and " *anxiety.*—His fight was difordered—he " thought there were numbers of flies " about him, and this made him uneafy.— " Why don't you kill thefe flies ?—he would " cry, with a great degree of impatience— " and then he would ftrike at them with his " hand, and would fhrink in the bed, as if " he were afraid of their getting to his face." —As the remedies ufed had been of no fervice, it was propofed to bleed him. This was done, to the amount of twenty ounces and upwards, in a full ftream, and with-

out

out producing the leaſt diſpoſition to faint,
or encreaſe ſickneſs—though the pulſe became thereby low, fluttering, and unequal.
—After V. S. the opiate was encreaſed;
and it was propoſed alſo to bathe his head
with vinegar, and towards evening, if he
was not better, to put him into the warm
bath.—But every ſymptom ſoon became
to ſuch a height as left no room to do
any thing—he became highly delirious—
he got a clyſter with half an ounce of laudanum, but it came away almoſt immediately.—Convulſions ſtrong—he died a little
after—with " a ſmile on his countenance."

Treatment of Dr. Liſter's patient.

JAMES CORTON of York, was bit on
the right hand. Between five and ſix weeks
after, the hydrophobic ſymptoms appeared.
Dr. Liſter firſt ſaw him on Monday, about
one o'clock, March 12th, 1682-3.—The
morning before, he took ſome diaſcordium
—ſome cordial water was ordered by his
apo-

apothecary, but he could not fwallow it.
The Doctor caufed a vein to be opened in the
arm that was bit, and directed " the wound
" to be fcarified, and drawn with vefecatories,
" and the fame plaifter to be applied to the
" neck and legs, and infide of the arms."—
The antidotes of the day were next had recourfe to:—" I ordered the ufual, and famed
" antidotes to be given him, as of theriaca,
" cinis cancrorum, ruta, agaricus, &c. in
" bolufes.—Of thefe bolufes he took a dram
" every hour, for at leaft a dozen of times."

TUESDAY " he had a violent fever upon
" him."—He refufed drink in every fhape
offered, whether through a quill, or otherwife—he foon after fell into a convulfive fit
—after it was over, " he took an elleborifm
" in a bolus, very willingly; it wrought
" about three or four times very plentifully,
" and he declared himfelf wonderfully re-
" lieved by it."—Four hours after, the
Doctor returned; he found the Minifter
with his patient, who prayed very earneftly
—talked

—talked with the Minifter *very fenfibly*—
and defired the facrament.—He foon after
died.

Treatment of Dr. Howman's patient.

THIS was a perfon at Norwich.—About
fix weeks after the bite, the fymptoms
made their appearance.—The Doctor was
called on Wednefday, October 1ft; 1684.—
" This morning he had taken (I know not
" by whofe advice," fays the Doctor) a dofe
" of the common fpirit of fcurvy-grafs,
" which gave him feven or eight ftools, and
" made him very faint.—I prefcribed," fays
the Doctor, " the beft temperate anti-
" fpafmodic and antiparalytic remedies I
" knew, to be mixed with the fpecifics
" of common ufe in an Hydrophobia."—
Next day, the left arm was bled—the quantity taken, about feven ounces; the other
arm, being the one bit, was paralytic :—
the remedies to be continued as before prefcribed.—The Doctor left him now.—No
Hydro-

Hydrophobia had yet appeared, but in his abfence, " the great *fymptom* appeared, and " another was confulted, who gave him " many remedies." The Doctor tells us, he returned from the country on Friday.— " *His reafon was all along very good,* and, as " fome obferved, better than in his health." —At ten this night all his fymptoms worfe. —He died between twelve and one next morning.

Treatment of Mr. Turner's patient.

THIS was a child of about three years of age. He was bit on the cheek, and im‑ mediately carried to Mr. Turner.—" The " wound we treated with digeftives for " fome time, *futures* were forborn, though " otherwife neceffary," (the wound was large) " that the *fanation* thereof being de‑ " ferred, the contracted venom might have " the freer *egrefs* thereat.—In about three " weeks time we had *incarned,* and brought " over a very firm, and feemly *cicatrix;*

B b   " and

" and in about two days after, the child
" was feized with a fever, &c."—Here
the Hydrophobia came on in lefs than
a month.—This is the earlieft cafe of its
appearance in the human fpecies of which
I remember to have read.—Next day the
little patient was in a moft deplorable way.
—Among other fymptoms, the eyes were
diftorted, and *there appeared* " an irregular
" expanfion of the optic nerve, attended
" with an *extraordinary fiercenefs,* in the
" whole vifage.". He could not bear the
reflection of a looking-glafs.—" In the
" evening, notwithftanding fuch *alexiphar-*
" *mics* as had been exhibited, he funk under
" the oppreffion of thefe cruel fymptoms."
—We are not told what thefe alexipharmics
were, but we may conclude they were fome
of the common fpecifics of the times.

Treat-

*Treatment of John Brown, thirteen years
of age, Dr. Dickson's patient.—The accident happened in January, 1767, in
Whitechapel-road, London.*

" He was immediately carried to the
" London hospital, where the parts affected,
" which were the right cheek and shoul-
" der, were very well scarified, and suffered
" to bleed freely. *Mercurial ointment* was
" rubbed on these parts immediately after-
" wards ; and this was done twice a day,
" for ten days, without producing any spit-
" ting, or even soreness of the gums."—He
left the hospital at the end of three weeks,
free from all complaints, after taking three
doses of purging salts.—On the 30th of
April, he felt symptoms of the disease, and
was again carried back to the hospital.—
The Doctor ordered the warm bath ; but it
was with great difficulty he could be pre-
vailed on to go into it.—After staying in it
a little, " he found his throat become quite
                                    " easy."

" eafy."—But he could not, without the utmoft difficulty, fwallow fome fpermaceti mixture, with a little Tinct. Theb. that was ordered him.—He plunged his head twice under the water by the Doctor's entreaty.—After this, he got down about an ounce of the fpermaceti mixture, containing twenty drops of Tinct. Theb.—Twenty drops of Tinct Theb. were now directed to be given every hour, in the fame mixture, if he could fwallow a liquid—or one grain of Extr. Theb.—if neither could be got down, **to** have a clyfter every two hours of a little broth and one dram of Tinct Theb, with fomentations frequently applied to the neck and throat, and an emolient poultice, if poffible.—He was laid in bed, and fweated half an hour very copioufly—He lay quite eafy under it—but he enjoyed only a fhort interval—every fymptom grew worfe.—No medicines could be given, except a pill of two grains of Extr. Theb.—this was about three o'clock.—He complained foon after this of hunger, and eat an apple greedily,

with

with a piece of bread and butter.—He took
two grains more of Extr. Theb. at fix he
vomited frequently—all his complaints encreafed—a dram and a half of Tinct. Theb.
was thrown up in a clyfter.—He died at
eleven this evening, continuing very fenfible
till within a quarter of an hour of his end.

Treatment of Dr. Mead's firft patient.

HE was a lad about nine years of age;
bit on the right cheek. A Surgeon cured
the wound, which was very large, in fourteen days, by applying, we are told, Theriac.
Androm. in Sp. Vin. and afterwards drefling
it with Linim. Arcæi, and Balf. Terebinth.

" No other care was taken, only a Bol.
" of Theriac. Androm. was given him every
" night while under cure; and, quickly
" after he was bit, he was perfuaded to *eat*
" *the whole liver of the dog.*"—Such was
the fpecific of that time.—" Bliftering plai-
" fters were applied to the back, and on
" each

" each fide of the neck ; and a diuretic Bol.
" of Camphor. Sal. Succin. and Conferv.
" Lujul. was given every fix hours."—
Next day, which was the fecond of his
difeafe, " he eat fome bread and butter
" heartily," but vomited it immediately up
again.—He was dipped in a tub of warm
water—and was quiet in it for a little while
but foon fell into a convulfive fit.—Every
fymptom now encreafed—he was toffed with
violence from one place to another—and
foon after expired.

Treatment of Dr. Mead's fecond patient.

HE was a man of forty-five. He was bit
in one of his fore fingers, near the nail, ten
weeks before.

WHEN the fymptoms appeared, the firft
thing thofe about him did, was to give him
a vomit of Rad. Ipecacuan.—On the fecond
day after, he had eight ounces of blood
taken from his arm; and took a Bol. of
Theriac.

Theriac. Androm. with Lap. Contraierv.
—It was not till the third day of his illnefs
the Doctor faw him. He found him then
tied in bed, and in the laft ftage of the difeafe.—" I obferved he had a palfy in his
" right arm."—His fight was alfo affected
—for " he had endeavoured to read, but
" could not, complaining of a mift before
" his eyes."—The Doctor ordered him to
be bled to the quantity of twenty ounces.—
Nothing more was done—this feemed to
reduce his ftrength greatly—and foon after
he expired.

DR. MEAD relates a third cafe of Hydrophobia, which was fent him by a Surgeon in Stamford, in Lincolnfhire; but
does not tell us what had been done, except that the wound was healed up by
Theriac. Androm. the common application
of thefe times: yet it had been long under
cure, for it was three months from the accident till Hydrophobia appeared, and then
there was left " a fmall black fcab behind."
The

The Surgeon, he tells us, opened the body, and flightly wounded his fore finger with his knife, " and was furprized to find that " it feftered, and gave him much more pain " than a greater cut at other times had " done.—This," fays the Doctor, " I the " rather take notice of, becaufe fomething " of the fame nature happened to the Sur- " geon who diffected my patient. His hand, " the following night, was taken with an " eryfepelas, attended with great heat, ten- " fion, and pain; this was owing to a little " wound made in one of his fingers a day " or two before, from which, in turning " over the parts, he had rubbed off the " plaifter."

Treatment of the Frenchwoman, bit by the fame dog that bit Mafter R. and only a few minutes before—by Mr. John Hun- ter.—The accident happened on the 6th of December, 1784.

MR. HUNTER in a letter writes me,— " The poor Frenchwoman the dog bit a " few

"few minutes before Mafter R. died laft
"Tuefday fe'nnight, at two o'clock in the
"morning. She was taken ill the Tuefday
"before with a pain in the wound, which
"rather encreafed. She called on me on
"the Thurfday, but I was not at home.
"She called on the Friday, and I faw
"her. The cicatrix was very painful,
"and fhe feemed not to be perfectly well.
"At twelve o'clock that evening, fhe was
"taken with a kind of fit. The apothecary
"was fent for, who gave her two grains of
"opium. I faw her on Saturday morning,
"when fhe had all the fymptoms of the
"difeafe, although not violent. I ordered
"opium to be given, as much as they could
"get her to take. The fymptoms became
"more and more till fhe died.

"FROM the time fhe took the firft dofe
"on Saturday about eleven o'clock, till fhe
"died, which was about fixty hours, fne
"took only forty-four grains of opium;

C c   "and

" and two hundred drops of. laudanum in
" clyfters.

" THE fores had cauftic applied feveral
" times, but *not till feveral days after the*
" *accident.*"

Dated London, April 2d, 1785.

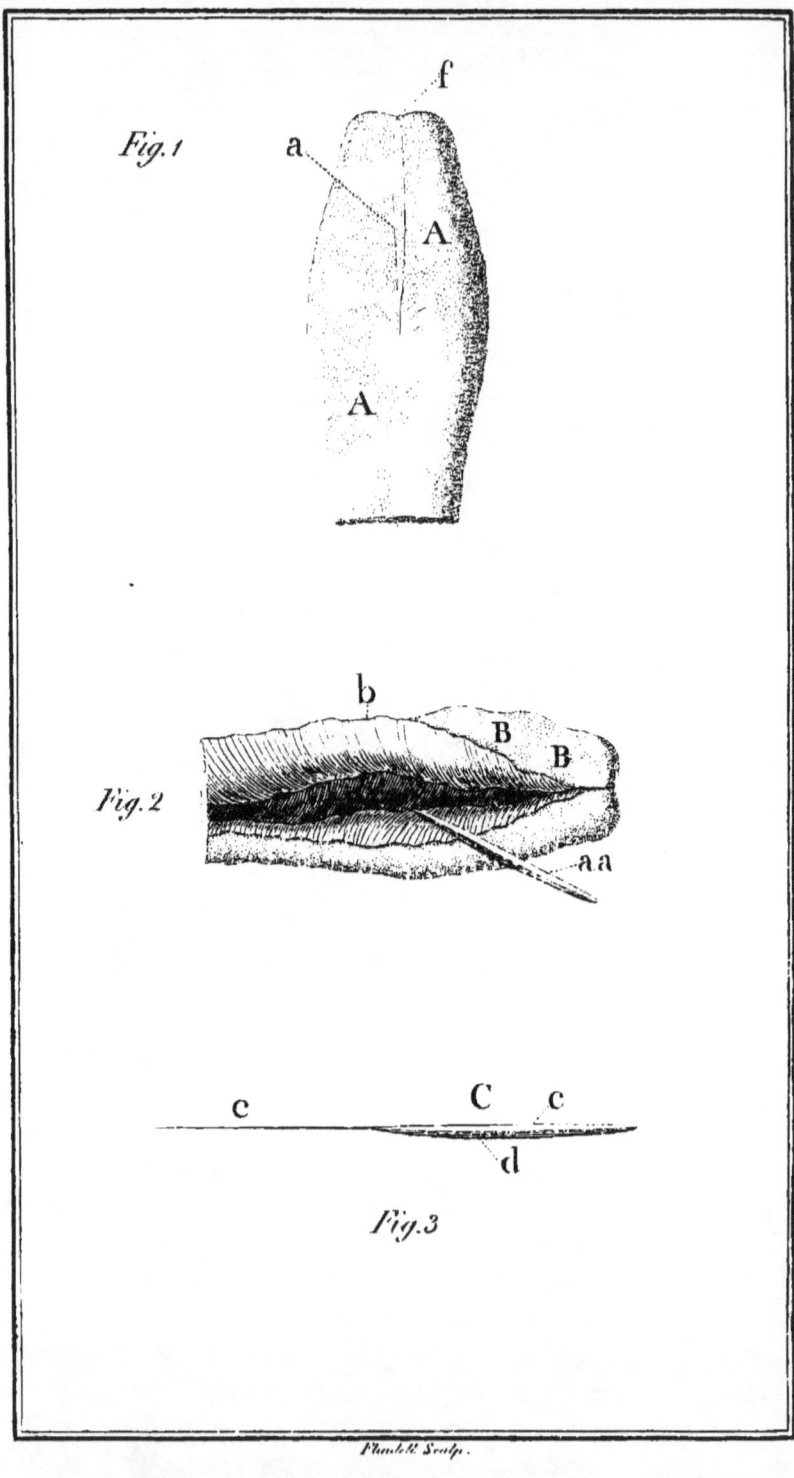

Fig. 1

Fig. 2

Fig. 3

EXPLANATION *of the* PLATE.

FIG. 1.

A. A. Part of the Tongue of a Dog; the under Side turned upwards, to shew the *Worm* in situ.

a. The Worm, as it appears through the Cuticle.

f. Its Communication with the marginal Line of the Tongue.

FIG. 2

B. B. The Tongue dissected.

b. The Cuticle separated, and laid back, to shew the Muscle wherein the Worm lies.

a. a. The Worm raised from its Situation, with its Attachment to the Muscle.

FIG. 3.

C. The Worm taken out.

c. The tendinous Part.

d. The ligamentous.

e. The ligamentous running out to a Point, but which unites and mixes with the muscular Fibres, so as to be lost among them.

APPENDIX.

The cafe of ——— Chrifty, admitted into the Royal Infirmary of Edinburgh, as taken down by the late Dr. Drummond, then Hofpital Clerk—and which, as far as I know, has never yet been publifhed.—Extracted from a MS of Mr. Rodolph Rhodes, Surgeon to the Firft regiment of Dragoon Guards, who alfo attended.

——— CHRISTY, aged eleven, was fix weeks ago bit on the right arm by a mad dog: nothing was done to the wound at the time. She has fince taken a medicine that contained liverwort for one of its ingredients: has been fweated for a confiderable time together, and taken fome mercurials.

ABOUT

ABOUT three days ago some unfavourable symptoms appeared. On Sunday at
one o'clock, P. M. she was taken into the
hospital, and had the cicatrices of her arm
cauterized, and took gr. v. of Vol. Alkali
in a bolus.

AT three she swallowed a second bolus of
the same, but not without much persuasion.
Starts sometimes, and seems much frightened; sighs frequently, and heavily; talks
in general sensibly, but sometimes raves;
pulse quick, and very irregular; is much
frightened if any cold touches her; starts,
and is more convulsed in a recumbent pos-
ture, than when she sits up.

AT four an attempt to go to stool. Is
afraid we shall shoot her; wishes to go to
sleep; pupils of her eyes very much dilated;
can bear the sight of a looking-glass, but
not even the mention of water. Another
bolus exhibited; she took it with more
reluct-

reluctance. At five, vomited. A fourth bolus given; and though her intention is evidently to take it, yet her arms feem, contrary to her inclination, to be convulfed, and thrown away from the mouth, when near it. Has difficulty in putting fugar to her mouth, of which fhe is fond. At eight, took another bolus of the Vol. Alk. and had a clyfter adminiftered, containing mufk fcrup. j. and L. L. gutt. xv.—did not retain it. Another bolus given at ten o'clock, confifting of mufk gr. x. and L. L. gutt. xv. but fhe rejected it immediately. Seeing it was impoffible to attempt another bolus, and from the bad fuccefs of the for-mer clyfter, L. L. gutt. xl. in aq. font. unc. du. was injected, but with much difficulty.

At half paft eleven o'clock all her former fymptoms encreafed. Cannot now bear the fight of a looking-glafs. Fits more fre-quent; convulfions ftronger; always rav-ing. Saliva from the mouth in great quan-tity, and appears bloody. Complains greatly
of

of her throat; has frequent reaching to vomit.

THREE o'clock, A. M. Has been raving conftantly fince our laft vifit. Conftant vomitting; flow of faliva more copious. At this time a bolus of mufk, gr. x. and L. L. gutt. xv. given, which fhe now took with much lefs reluctance than the former; but it did not feem to get beyond the larynx; it was vomited up the next moment.

FOUR o'clock. Took another bolus, and feemed as if fhe could retain it: fymptoms as before.—Half after five; ftill raves continually; but fometimes makes fenfible anfwers. Not fo much convulfed of late; nor feems fo much frightened. Made fome water. Has juft taken a bolus with little entreaty; and without the convulfed motion of her head as before.

HALF paft fix. Is now in a perfect fweat over her whole body. Pulfe rather
calmer,

calmer, but ſtill too indiſtinct to be reckoned.—Seven o'clock. More delirious;
weaker; convulſive ſtartings leſs frequent;
pulſe irregular, and weaker. Bolus rejected,
which ſhe ſwallowed with as little entreaty
as the laſt. Some moiſture ſtill on her ſkin,
but chiefly on the upper part of her body,
and of a clammy nature.—Half after eight
o'clock. Still weaker. Eyes very much
contorted; pupils exceſſively dilated.

Nine o'clock.—Sinks apace. Is now
without motion.—Dead. A little after
death the pupils contracted to nearly their
natural ſize.

DISSECTION.

I. The whole ſurface of the body of a
dun colour. Nails livid; alſo ſome parts
of the arms.

II. Head. D. mater of the natural
appearance. Nothing extraordinary in the
ven-

ventricles. Choroid plexus rather pale;
Veins on the furface, as ufual, diftended
with blood.

III. Fauces. Membrane lining the infide of the mouth of the natural colour:
Tongue alfo natural. Epiglottis, larynx,
and fpaces between the cartilages of the
Trachea; fo very little altered as to render it
doubtful whether any thing redder than
common. Pharynx natural. Submaxillary
glands of the natural appearance. Parofids
being cut through appeared redder, but
doubtful whether the rednefs did not proceed from extravafation of blood from the
cut veffels.

IV. Thorax. Œfophagus natural.
Lungs much inflamed; and, towards the
back part, of a livid appearance. Pericar-
dium, and furface of the heart natural. A
confiderable foft whitifh polypus in the
right auricle, adhering loofely. Right ven-
tricle no blood. Smaller polypus than that

in

in the right auricle found in the left auricle, and adhering rather more firmly. Little red blood in the heart.

V. ABDOMEN. Stomach natural. Some mucus in it. Two lumbrici. That part of the inteſtines towards the end of the ilium contracted, and the coats thickened in ſome places. Pancreas redder than uſual. All other parts found.

A caſe of Hydrophobia communicated to me by Mr. Tuſon, Surgeon, at Boxford.— The accident happened Dec. 6th, 1784. —The ſubject of the caſe, Maſter R. already alluded to in theſe pages.

I WAS informed he was on a viſit in Jermyn-ſtreet, the 6th of December, 1784, where a ſtray dog came into the room. The lady of the houſe taking notice of its being very thin and poor, ordered a plate of meat to be ſet before it, which the dog eat. The young gentleman took particular notice of

D d

it

it, and ftooping down to examine it, the animal turned from its meat, and bit him on the right fide of the lower lip. He was immediately fent in a coach, which was then ready at the door, to Mr. Hunter's in Leicefter-fields, being at the diftance of about a quarter of a mile, who very wifely and cautioufly treated it as fuppofing the dog mad, by applying a cauftic to the part, in fuch manner as to endeavour to deftroy all the adjacent abforbing veffels from taking up any of the venom. Immediately on which Dr. Turton was confulted. The Ormf-kirk medicine was given, and mercurial ointment rubbed into the legs twice a day; the mufk medicine was likewife given.

I FOUND by Dr. Turton's account, they were alarmed at the feel of the fkin, and fome other dangerous fymptoms, when in town, before the mufk medicine was given. They continued the Tonquin medicine and ointment till he came into the country, which was on the 24th of December, where

he

he arrived in perfect health. I saw him on
the 25th, with his lip healed, which was
kept open till nearly the time he came
down. I received directions from Dr. Turton and Mr. Hunter as follows: That
" the general health must be more parti-
" cularly attended to, the state of the bow-
" els, the pulse, &c. must be watched."—
Before he began the musk medicines, the
pulse was low and feeble, the feel of the
skin cold and clammy, though he made no
complaints.—The feel of the skin and pulse
are now (25th) much better; and he appears
to have no complaints.—Bowels in their
natural state. Mr. Hunter thinks the
wound in the lip may be permitted to heal,
and that any little softening application,
such as suet, oil, fresh butter, &c. and pre-
serving it from the air, is all that may be
necessary.—" We wish, however, not to
" omit any thing that may be necessary to
" prevent mischief, and could wish the
" musk medicine and mercurial ointment
" to be continued, under the direction of
" those

" thofe who attend. Half a dram of the
" ftrong mercurial ointment may be rubbed
" in twice a day, but the gums and mouth
" muft be watched, as we do not wifh to
" bring on a falivation, though we could
" wifh to fill the conftitution pretty full of
" mercury. Under this idea it muft be
" continued or difcontinued, from time to
" time, for three weeks to come.

" WE fhould advife, alfo, the ufe of the
" following prefcription, according to the
" circumftances of the pulfe and feel of the
" fkin, and *general ftate of health*, which we
" beg to repeat, as we confider it as the
" moft material."

Two fcruples of the ftrong mercurial
ointment were rubbed in for two or three
days; but as the weather has been fo fevere,
half a dram only hath been ufed twice a day,
and that difcontinued for two or three days,
The mufk medicine, as ordered, was

R. Mofch.

" R. Mofch. gr. vj.—Cinnab. fact. &
" nat. aa gr. viij.—Ft. Bol. 8vo. quaq; hor.
" fumendus."—For fome days he hath only
taken it twice a day.—" The dofe of mufk
" and cinnabar may be varied according to
" circumftanees, but fhould be continued,
" at times, for three weeks to come."

I WAS, on enquiry, informed the dog
was fecured, and died before the young gentleman left town ; therefore, I obferved a
ftrict attention to the method adopted of
giving the mufk medicine, and rubbing in
half a dram of the ftrong mercurial ointment twice a day : I was defired to vifit him
every other day. He continued perfectly
well as to his pulfe, feel of the fkin, ftate
of the bowels, and in great fpirits, till about
four days after, when I perceived a cold
clammy feel on the hands, with a tolerable
good pulfe, but without complaint. I was
induced to believe that this feel might arife
from a pain from a contufion on his great
toe,

toe, which was occafioned by a table being overturned and falling upon it.. Upon my next vifit, I found that difagreeable fymptom quite gone off; his hands very warm, dry, and comfortable, and his toe much eafier, which feemed to confirm my fufpicion.

As I wifhed to prevent any bad confequences as much as poffible, and adhere to Dr. Turton's ideas, about fix or feven days after his coming into the country, I encreafed the dofes of mufk to eight grains, and the cinnabar to ten each, and the ointment to two fcruples twice a day. In this manner he proceeded till January 12th, without any fymptom of illnefs or complaint whatever. I was as particular and minute as poffible in my examinations, and could not find any tendency in his conftitution but what perfectly coincided with health.—I was fent for early on Wednefday morning 12th January, and, upon my arrival, was informed, that the young gentleman

man had complained about four o'clock in the afternoon of the day before, with head-ach and ficknefs, that he had a very reftlefs night, and at this time could not fwallow well. I was alarmed at the account, and forry, as I vifited him every other day, that he happened to be feized on my vacant day. Upon my entering the room, I immediately perceived he laboured under a confirmed Hydrophobia. I called for fomething for him to drink: as foon as it was offered him, he was immediately convulfed, particularly about the throat, and drank it with much agitation: this confirmed me in my opinion. He complained exceedingly of a pain in his head, and great thirft; his pulfe was very quick, full, and hard; and he lay toffing about in the bed. I afked him if he felt any uneafinefs in his lip. He told me he felt pricking pains about the part the evening before, and at that time he felt a forenefs on touching it. I defired that every affiftance that could might be procured. Two meffengers were

dif-dispatched for two Physicians. In the interim, I gave him three doses of the above musk medicines every hour, and proposed bleeding him; but as farther assistance had been sent for, I deferred it till they came: they agreed in my opinion. I took about ten ounces of blood from the arm; they wished to see him take some liquid; he took it in his hand, put it hastily to his mouth, and upon deglutition, all the muscles concerned in that action seemed very much convulsed. His tongue appeared clean, not dry. They ordered him—R. Cinnab. nat. & fact. aa gr. viij—Mosch. gr. decem.—Opii. gr. j.—Conserv. Cynosbat. gr. ij. Syr. q. s. ft. pil. ij.—Statim. sumend. & tert. quaq; hor. repetend. sine Opio. These he took regularly; likewise an injection with a pint of gruel, and two ounces of oil, thrown up for a clyster. A cloth wetted with oil was applied to his throat: his feet bathed with flannels dipped in hot water for a considerable time together, and four scruples of the strong mercurial ointment

was

was rubbed in twice a day, as they wifhed to promote a ptialifm. He paffed moft of the day in a chair, and now and then walked about the room. His eyes appeared very wild and red. He had a fmall ftool from the ufe of the injection. He made very little urine; his blood appeared a little inflamed, and fomewhat fizy. In the courfe of the day he frequently took bread moiftened in tea or gruel. He went to bed in the evening early, and got two or three hours fleep (I fuppofe from the effect of the grain of opium) after which he appeared very reftlefs, and convulfed; towards the morning he was exceedingly fo, and not able to lie ftill a moment, conftantly calling for fomething to drink, and complaining of great thirft. He then fwallowed with great anxiety and perturbation, and appeared in the utmoft diftrefs. On the morning of the 13th (Thurfday) he rofe about ten o'clock in the ftate above mentioned; about twelve his phyficians faw him again: his pulfe was about one hundred and thirty. They then ordered

E e him

him—R. Mofch. gr. xij.—Mercur. Emet;
flav. gr. ij.—Opii. gr. j.—Mucilag. G. Arab.
q. f. ut ft. Pil. No. ij. tert.—quaq; hor;
repetend. cum, vel fine opio. prout res
poftulare videatur,—and continue the ufe
of the ointment.—They had not left him
an hour, before he was taken with frequent
vomitings, reachings, and conftantly fpitting a vifcid phlegm. This came on before
he took the Turbith pills. He took one
dofe with opium as foon as it came, which
was about two o'clock. He was very fenfible and pertinent in his anfwers and converfation till now, when a delirium came on,
with fuch fears and horrors as are fcarcely
defcribable—rubbing his throat, and walk-
ing up and down the room in great agony,
but without any violence to any one in it.
He continued in this diftreffed ftate till about
fix in the evening, when he was ftanding up,
and leaning on the houfekeeper, and nature,
from his inceffant talking and raving, being
exhaufted, he dropped down in a kind of
fit. He was then laid on a bed quite fenfelefs,

lefs and fpeechlefs, groaning, foaming at
the mouth, now and then vomiting a dark
brown choler, and appeared as if ftrangled.
He expired about half paft eleven at night.
His lip, after death, did not appear altered.

It fhould have been mentioned, that on
the 11th he complained greatly of a pain in
his right ear—and this was the firft fymptom obferved.—A flannel dipped in warm
water was applied, to which was added a
little brandy: by this method the pain
abated in the afternoon of Wednefday the
12th.

The following letter I received from Mr.
Hunter in the beginning of March;
fome paragraphs of which have already
been quoted.

Sir,

I received the favour of yours. I am
always extremely happy when I can give
any ufeful information; but all the information

mation I can give you relative to the Hydrophobia is rather negative good than pofitive. All the means recommended were
ufed in Mafter R.'s cafe. I faw him only
a few hours after the bite. The lip was
torn a good deal. The teeth had gone
through and through, and had torn out a
piece. I immediately applied the cauftic
to every furface that I conceived had been
made by the dog's teeth; and when thofe
floughs came away, I went over the fame
field a fecond time; but, from the termi-
nation of the whole, I am inclinable to believe that I did not touch every part where
the teeth had been. He took the Ormfkirk
medicine by the direction of Mr. Barry
who fells it, therefore we muft fuppofe it
was properly given. He alfo took the Tonquin medicine, viz. mufk, cinnabar, &c.
as alfo rubbed in mercurial ointment till
his mouth was fore. My whole depend-
ance was on the cauftic, but did not object
to the others being given. I wifh I could
fay more on the fubject in general. We
feem

ſeem to be as much at a loſs how to treat it as they were a thouſand years ago. I have not yet heard of the particulars of Maſter R.'s attack and ſymptoms. I want very much to learn them. To aſcertain a mode of cure will be very difficult. For a few caſes not having the ſymptoms, under any courſe, prove but little. I know where there were twenty-one people bit by one dog; nothing was done for any of them, and only one was taken ill. If they had all taken medicines, then it would have been ſaid, that they only loſt one out of twenty-one.

I am, dear Sir,

Your moſt obedient ſervant,

JOHN HUNTER.

The

*The following was sent me by Mr. Newson,
an ingenious Surgeon in Woodbridge.*

To Dr. HAMILTON.

DEAR SIR,

As the following case of the bite of a
mad dog was succefsfully treated, doubtlefs
it will be acceptable to you, as a fupport to
that fyftem of advice you moft judicioufly
recommend, and which, in my opinion, is
is the only known prophylactic method at
prefent that any perfon can place any rational confidence in, as a fecurity from the
moft direful effects of a difeafe by much the
worft to which human nature is fubject.

EIGHT years ago laft Auguft, during the
time I was affiftant to a Surgeon, in Norfolk,
of great eminence and real fkill, the alarming cafe of the bite of a mad dog came
under my infpection. It took place in confequence

fequence of a favourite dog being rabidly
infected, and from lofing his hilarity, and
accuftomed fondnefs for his mafter, and
being obferved to fkulk beneath a table,
the fervant maid was requefted to take him
out and feed him, and in endeavouring
to withdraw him, received a confiderable
bite from him in the flefhy part of her arm.
The laceration extended in circumference
not lefs than four inches; as near as I can
recollect, the whole part was removed within two hours of the melancholy accident;
by excifion, and at leaft half an inch deeper,
and wider than the dog's teeth had penetrated or extended. The wound was afterwards dreffed with efcharotics, viz. red præcipitate of mercury fprinkled on lint, and a
large cataplafm of oil, milk, and bread, applied over the whole part. It was dreffed
again the fame evening, and repeated many
days, which brought off feveral fmall efchars,
and a great difcharge was excited, and kept
paffing off a confiderable time. The wound

was

was kept open for fix or feven weeks, and cicatrized without any difficulty. She like-wife took Turbith mineral, night and morning; and, in the intermediate time, fome of the moſt eſteemed antiſpaſmodic medicines were adminiſtered, ſuch as muſk, caſtor, valerian, aſſa fœtida, and opiates; after which the bark, in ſubſtance; and finiſhed with the cold bath.

THE dog that gave her the bite was evidently mad, as two other dogs were bit by him foon after. They were fecured, and within eight or nine days difcovered the ſtrongeſt figns of genuine madneſs.— I think the event of this cafe manifeſtly declares, and proves, the juſtice of the proceeding and treatment this girl underwent, viz. from not receiving any hurt; from the dog being indiſputably mad; and the perfon bitten had not the chance of efcaping free from infection from the dog's teeth having been wiped, by previouſly paſſ-

ing

ing through any clothing, fo as to take off the fubtle and active matter.

I am, dear Sir, with refpect,

Your obliged and

Obedient humble fervant,

JOHN NEWSON.

The following appeared in the Ipfwich Journal of February 19.

To Dr. H.

SIR,   Feb. 17, 1785.

YOUR very learned and intelligent differ-tation in the laft Ipfwich Journal, upon the treatment and effects of the bite of a MAD DOG has given me not only great pleafure, but much information, and has encouraged me to trouble the printer and you with the mode of treatment two men underwent, a few years fince, that were bitten by a mad dog, and were under my directions.—

F f   The

The part bitten was immediately fcarified, and a ftrong cauftic, of at leaft the fize of the wound, was applied, which produced a very deep efchar; upon the removal of which, the wound was dreffed with red præcipitate, or Egyptian ointment, conftantly, to keep up as large a difcharge as poffible, and prevent the wounds healing, which they were not allowed to do for many weeks. The patients each took five or fix dofes of the Ormfkirk powder, and as many of the Tonquin; but, having a fufpicious opinion of thofe *once* celebrated remedies, I ordered a fufficient quantity of mercurial ointment to be rubbed into the bitten leg, fo as to faturate the body without occafioning a fpitting. The patients were ordered a light, though not very low, diet, and their fpirits kept up as much as poffible, by every art in my power, both by forbidding their friends talking on the fubject, and by my promifes of (what indeed I doubted) the infallibility of the means put in practice.—That the dog was mad

ad-

admitted of no difpute, as the animals bitten by him, on the fame day my patients
were, died mad; yet my friends had the
good fortune to efcape, without one alarming fymptom, notwithftanding both their
legs bled from the bite, and one had his
pretty much torn.—This is a true and exact
narrative of the cafes and treatment, and it
would be an additional favour to me and
the public, if Dr. H. would be kind enough
to make his free comments upon both, that
future unhappy fellow-creatures, under fimilar misfortunes, may reap the benefit of
his learning and philanthropy.   G.

P. S. I am apprehenfive, that although
different *poifons* fhew their *effects* at different periods, yet the *caufe* is fooner communicated to the animal juices than Dr. H.
has hinted; and that, notwithftanding you
cut out the *local puftule*, occafioned by the
inoculating fcarification, on the fifth, fixth,
or feventh day, ftill you will not eradicate
the fmall-pox from the fyftem.

Ex-

Extract of a letter from Mr. Goodwin,
dated Earl-Soham, Feb. 28, 1785.

——'Tis a fair thing to fay, that ninety-
nine out of a hundred reputed mad dogs,
are not really fo; but are loft by their
mafters, and hunted by the vulgar into a
frenzy; or are delirious from fevers, to
which they are very fubject; and, I think,
are capable of inoculating that fever on their
own fpecies, when they are not upon the
human.

You are perfectly right refpecting *worm-*
ing dogs, notwithftanding the plaufible ad-
drefs on that matter lately. It is impoffible
removing the tendon from the tongue can
prevent the dog's running away when mad.
But vulgar opinions, though having no
foundation in truth, are impoffible to be
removed; witnefs the prejudices in Lan-
cafhire in favour of the Ormfkirk powder.
I once lived there, was intimate with
Hill,

Hill, and believe, many a man might have been found, who would have received the bite of a mad dog for hire, from the belief of the infallibility of that medicine; which now is fo much exploded. The truth is, fo very few of the reputed mad dogs are really fo, that any medicine, with quackery, may be rendered popular; but, I much fear, no remedy is yet found for the bite of a mad dog, on the *nakea* body, but almoft immediate excifion : I fay naked, as I believe many fubjects have owed their efcape more from their clothes, than their Doctor. The faliva of the dog, being naturally thick, is apt to be ftrained by the ftocking, &c.

THE time of poifons fhewing their effects, depends on various caufes :—the nature of the poifon itfelf; the time of the year; the patient's habit—all have an influence. Yet, I think, excifion muft *foon* be performed, or the venom will have travelled beyond the knife. The viper's poifon is almoft inftan-

taneous

taneous in its effects.—A lad I looked after was bitten on his finger, and in a *few minutes* fell into violent vomitting and purging.—Another, bitten in both legs, *directly* fwelled all over, with fo great a difficulty of breathing, I thought of nothing but fuffocation. Thefe are mentioned to fhew the fpicula and nature of the venom, and to beg the favour of your turning your attention that way. As the minds of many people may be inflamed by the recent misfortune in this neighbourhood, and many made wretched that may happen to be bitten, I hope, and make no doubt, but your publication will tend to alleviate their anxiety, by fhewing the great odds againft their being bitten by a *real mad* dog; and then, the probable chance of efcape, by the faliva or venom being left upon their clothes.

I am refpectfully, dear Sir,

Your obliged humble fervant,

WM. GOODWIN.

SYMP-

SYMPTOMS.

In the following, the reader will find collected the moſt material of the SYMP-TOMS that appeared in the caſes alluded to.

Dr. Mead's three patients.—Vid. Philoſ. Tranſact. No. 323.

SYMPTOMS *in the firſt.*

THE patient was a lad about nine years of age. From the 20th of April, when bit, till the 22d of May, continued well. On this day, ſeemed dull, and ſick; would eat no dinner; in the evening complained of his ſtomach and head; in the night very bad; ſtarted often, and ſcreamed out—re-fuſed drink—complained greatly when he made urine, ſaying it hurt him.—Next morning (23d) vomited—in the afternoon, ſweated; trembling; toſſing himſelf up

and

and down; talking continually; looking very wild; pulfe low; fometimes quicker, fometimes flower; urine appeared of a natural colour; could not fwallow.—Next day (24th) much worfe; could not bear the fight of any thing white; became convulfed; eyes grew more ftaring; pupils prodigioufly enlarged; convulfions fo violent, that it was with difficulty he was kept in bed; at length became tired and fpent; fell into cold fweats; and died in this way at four in the afternoon.

Second Patient.

SYMPTOMS.

THE patient a very lufty vigorous man of forty-five. On the 8th of November in the morning, *i. e.* ten weeks from the bite, complained of great ficknefs at ftomach; vomiting green and yellow choler.—Next morning (9th) began to complain of a difficulty in fwallowing; took drink with much difficulty.—On the 11th the Doctor

firft

firſt ſaw him, it ſeems :—was then tied in bed, raving mad; biting and ſpitting at the by-ſtanders; crying out murder; making an odd noiſe, as if he coughed up ſome-thing from the throat.—This, the Doctor adds, is, as he ſuppoſes, what ſome authors call barking.—Was untied, but ſoon became ſo unruly that it was with difficulty he was tied again.—Palſy of his right arm—this ſymptom appeared on the 10th, *i. e.* the day before; complained then alſo of a miſt before his eyes—ſeemed afraid of every body.—Was to-day blooded; then was quiet for a few minutes; but ſoon his outrageous fit returned, and he laid himſelf down, quite ſpent, and died.

Third Patient.

SYMPTOMS.

THIS patient was a young man of eigh-teen, the Doctor tells us; and adds, that, three days before his death, he was ſeized with a fever, for which he was blooded, vomited, and bliftered : he bit to pieces the glafs in which drink was given him.—During the whole violence of the diftemper, the penis was obferved to be conftantly erected, and as hard as a bone.

THESE are all the fymptoms the Doctor relates in this cafe; but, in his account of the diffection, he adds the following anecdote, viz. that the Surgeon who was employed to open the body, flightly wounded his fore finger, and was furprized to find it gave him much more pain than a greater cut at other times had done.—" This," he fays, " I the rather take notice of, be-" caufe fomething of the fame nature hap-" pened to the Surgeon who diffected my " patient. His hand, the following night, " was taken with an eryfepelas attended " with great heat, tenfion, and pain. This " was owing to a little wound made in one " of his fingers a day or two before, from " which, in turning over the parts, he had " rubbed off the plaifter; and it went not " off

" without the application of cooling and
" difcutient medicines."

*Cafe by Mr. De La Pryme.—Vid. Philof.
Tranfact. No. 277.*

SYMPTOMS.

THE patient aged fourteen.—Is not faid to
have been bit, but only to have frequently
put his finger into the throat of a whelp,
when they found it could not fwallow, to
fee what ailed it. The mother of this, and
fome other whelps, was bit by a mad dog;
became mad, as did all the whelps, in
about three weeks after, except this one.—
After fome time longer, this alfo fhewed
figns of the difeafe, and, in a day or
two more, died.—The firft fymptoms in
this boy were—Pain in the head—fomewhat
feverifh; and continued better and worfe
for fome time. Had a cough; eat hearty,
yet could not drink.—The fenfation of the
cold air gave him great uneafinefs—" he
" ran from it," as it is expreffed, " as if
" it

" it had been to fave his life"; and faid,
" that the wind would needs ftop his
" breath."—In a day or two more, became
worfe; vomited a matter like black blood,
" which ftunk like fallad oil, but much
" ftronger; after which he would be pretty
" well, and walk about, but moft com-
" monly ran as faft as he could, firft out of
" one corner, then into another—then up
" ftairs, then down again; as if it was for
" his life."—On the third day of his con-
finement, grew perfectly mad—would ftart,
leap, and twift his arms together.—His fits
were now fo ftrong, that four men could
hardly hold him.—Wanted to bite—ftrug-
gled fome time longer—and became fpeechlefs—and, it is added, " then died, juft as
" the Phyfician came."

*Symptoms in Dr. Munckley's patient.—
Vid. Med. Tanfact. Vol. II. p. 46.*

THE patient thirty-fix years of age. Bit
by one of his hounds, in his own ftables,

on

on the 11th of July, 1760.—On the 19th
of Auguſt, felt a difficulty in ſwallowing,
reſembling what proceeds from a common
ſore throat.—His friends had obſerved
him melancholy for ſome time.—Next
day the Doctor found him in bed.—" He
" was lying on his left ſide, and reſting
" his head, a little lifted up from the pil-
" low, upon one hand.—He had in his
" countenance the appearance of a fixed
" melancholy, and did not care to lift up
" his eyes," on being deſired to anſwer
queſtions.—No conſiderable degree of heat.
—Pulſe low—not much quicker than in
health.—Veſſels of the eyes appeared turgid.
—Tongue parched and dry, not white.—
On the word drink being mentioned, ſtarted
almoſt upright in bed, and put on the look
of fierceneſs and anger—repeating with great
eagarneſs and quickneſs, the word *drink !*—
ſaying it was impoſſible to drink—" and
" begged for God's ſake I would not men-
" tion it."—A very ſhort time before, *i. e.*
leſs than an hour, he had no ſymptom of this
ſort.—

īort.—Here we may fee how quickly the
aquæ pavor comes on.—Slept none this
night, yet lay quiet.—Towards morning,
however, began to fhew figns of great uneafinefs and diftrefs.—Thefe gradually encreafed, till about ten o'clock, when they
had arrived to fo great a height, that none of
his friends could bear to remain with him.

TEN o'clock.—Sitting up in his bed,
with an attendant on each fide.—In great
agitation of body; tofling his arms from
fide to fide; and moving himfelf about with
great vehemence.—His eyes were redder
than the day before.—He bared now one of
his arms, and ftriking it with all his force,
cried out to the Phyfician, with great eager-
nefs, to order him to be let blood.—" In
" his looks were the appearance of horror
" and defpair, beyond what," fays the Doctor, " I had ever feen before, either in
madnefs, or any other kind of delirium."—
Spat much; fometimes to the top of the
bed; at other times about the room; fometimes

times into the handkerchiefs which the attendants had for that purpofe.—The phlegm which he fpat was of a yellow caft; fo tenacious, that it was with difficulty got up: hence, when he opened his mouth, it could be feen adhering to the roof; but no foam about the mouth.—The found which he made in endeavouring to raife the phlegm, was of a very fingular kind—it was different from common hawking.—This found varied alfo at different times, being at fome times much fharper than at others,—" and being frequently re- " peated," it is added, " and quick and " fudden, as every other motion of his body " was, a warm imagination might confider " it as barking or yelping like a dog." —Was perfectly in his fenfes at this time —knew every body—did not attempt to fnap or bite at any one, nor any thing within his reach.—On the collar of his fhirt being unbuttoned, the fore part of his neck appeared remarkably protuberant, and as

if

if the uppermoſt cartilages of the wind-
pipe had been ſwollen, and thruſt forward.

ONE of the attendants, who was a man that
had been much employed in the care of mad
people, held his left hand in one of his own,
and with the other gently ſtroked the out-
ſide of his throat; which ſeemed to give
him a momentary relief. This perſon was
deſired to be upon his guard; for it was
not impoſſible, but that he might receive a
bite; and that he ought to put on gloves,
or cover his hands in ſome way or other; if
he continued to be thus employed. But
he refuſed to do any thing of this kind;
and ſaid, that he had ſeen enough of him
in the courſe of the night, to be very certain
that there was nothing to be feared from
him. When the phlegm was ſo tough,
and tenacious, that the patient could not
himſelf ſpit it out of his mouth, this perſon put his fingers into his mouth, and
with the corner of an handkerchief drew it
out for him.—When water was brought
near,

near, and poured from one bafon to another;
it gave him the greateft diftrefs and horror ;
he feemed as if convulfed all over—fhrinked
from the fight—then called out aloud to the
perfon that poured the water in this way,
adding the word *villain,* and exclaiming
againft the cruelty of this treatment.—Died
about two that afternoon.

Three Cafes by Dr. Dickfon.

Firft Cafe.

SYMPTOMS.

JOHN BROWN, aged thirteen, bit, with
a great many more, in Whitechapel-Road.

APRIL 30th, felt a pain in the right
cheek, the part bitten, all of a fudden.—
Slept none this night ; yet eat his victuals.
—Next morning (Friday) eat his breakfaft;
in the evening could neither eat nor drink.
—Pains and cramp in his throat and cheek
returned with great violence and frequency.

H h   —Breath-

—Breathing became very difficult.—By Monday, May 4th, all his complaints encreaſed.—He had a wild, frighted, frightening ſtare—was very reſtleſs, ſhifting from place to place—hung his chin on his breaſt —great diſcharge of viſcid ſaliva, which he ſpat out with force to a conſiderable diſtance —could not bear the leaſt air to blow on his throat and cheek—a conſiderable mucous diſcharge from his noſtrills—breathing quick and laborious; pulſe ſoft, and not frequent.—Felt like a lump in his throat, but without ſoreneſs.—Was quite ſenſible.—Refuſed water; yet attempted it; and had a difficulty in bringing the glaſs to his mouth: it was done in the manner of one labouring under Chorea Sancti Viti.— Still complains of the cold air giving him great pain.—After the warm bath, a reſpite and a copious ſweat; but the ſpaſms and pain in the cheek returned.—Now, great reſtleſſneſs.—In ſome time after, was ſeized with conſiderable vomiting—the matter thrown up, frothy and colourleſs.—Vomiting con-

tinued

tinued frequent.—All his complaints encreafed. He continued very fenfible till
near a quarter of an hour before his death,
which happened at eleven o'clock at night.
—Dr. Dickfon takes notice, that fo great
was the reftleffnefs, that it was not in the
power of thofe who attended him to keep
the bed-clothes on him : he was at laft
ftrapped down.—It did not appear that light
any wife affected him, though the cold air
did.—Complained greatly of thirft, but
could not drink.—His fpitting of frothy
matter encreafed fo much, that, in fpite of
all the care poffible, his bed was exceedingly
wetted by it.—The mucous difcharge from
his nofe continued.—He never attempted
to bite any perfon ; but, half an hour before he died, being preffed by the apothecary to take a pill, he looked furious, and
feemed as if he aimed at ftriking him.—He
did not bark like a dog; though the nurfe
and the patients of the ward faid that he
made a noife like a young puppy.—His
pulfe could not be felt for five or fix hours
before

before his death.—The fpafms of his throat
became much more frequent, and the mufcles of the throat greatly affected, attended
with a very quick laborious breathing.

Second Cafe.

SYMPTOMS.

A GARDENER's fervant, bit by the fame
dog.—On April 28th, at a public-houfe,
after having drank fhare of feveral pots of
beer, he found, all at once, he could not
fwallow.—He had filled his mouth with
beer, but not being able to get down a
fingle drop, he fpurted it out with great
force, and cried out that he was a dead
man.—He thenceforth kept continually
fpitting a frothy matter, of which he defired thofe about him to beware.—Was exceedingly reftlefs.—Had no fleep; but remained perfectly fenfible till his death, on
Friday noon, May 1ft.

Third

Third Case.

SYMPTOMS.

—— BEAN, aged fixty-nine, at the end of three weeks and five days, was feized with a pain in the part bit, which extended to his throat.—His breathing became very fhort.—Next morning he drank fome tea, with difficulty.—Was delirious from this time till Thurfday fe'nnight following, when he died.—He fpat much frothy matter the whole time; and neither ate nor drank any thing fince the tea already mentioned, till ten minutes before his death, when he drank a cupful of cold tea.—He had no fleep during all his illnefs, and was blind the laft four days.

Cafe by Mr. Bathie of Fifeſhire, commu-
nicated to Dr. Hope.—Vid. Med. Com.
Vol. III. p. 290.

Symptoms.

James Patton, aged fourteen, was
bit on the back of his right hand on the
8th of November, 1774.—Continued well
till February 9th, 1775, or about eleven
weeks.—On this day, was attacked with
univerſal laſſitude; loathing of food; ſlight
head-ach : yet went to-day to his employ-
ment.—Next day (10th) went likewiſe to
his buſineſs of driving the plough.—Very
inactive and heavy to-day : his maſter re-
buked him for lazineſs, not knowing he
ailed any thing.—He complained now of a
pain between the elbow of the hand bit
and his ſhoulder; a diſorder of his throat,
and head-ach; could not now ſwallow liquids, from ſomething in his throat which
interrupted its paſſage : went this evening
from his maſter's to the houſe of his parents,

rents, which is about a mile; was fatigued by it, and faintifh; was feized foon after with a fhivering; and complained greatly of the pain of his arm and throat.—It may be worth while to remark, that his mother examined his arm, and obferved, that between the fhoulder top, and down towards the elbow, the fkin was of a yellow hue, having the appearance and feel of that of a dead perfon.—Got very little reft this night; conftantly fhifting from fide to fide, being in every pofture remarkably uneafy; and often attempting to drink, without effect.

SATURDAY (11th) continued much the fame; rather worfe than better.—He tried to fip out of a tea-fpoon; as foon as the liquid touched his fauces, it feemed at the peril of his life, fo ftrongly was he threatened with fuffocation.—Had this evening a paroxifm, refembling an intermittent: firft univerfal coldnefs and fhivering, fucceeded by a hot fit, and this by a fweating fit.—

Pain

Pain of the arm and throat now diffufed all over his body.

ABOUT the middle of the night, was feized with delirium.—Struck his mother, who waited by, imagining fhe was fome other perfon intending him mifchief; but when fhe reafoned with him calmly, he became fenfible of his miftake, and was forry for his behaviour.—After this attack, he took little notice of any perfon, unlefs when he was fpoke to; had now a timid look; was eafily alarmed with noife, or the prefentation of luminous objects; had a fubfultus tendinum, and raved much; but when afked queftions relative to his health, he immediately appeared awake and collected, and gave diftinct and fenfible anfwers, returning foon into his reverie as before, when permitted to be undifturbed.— Even to the conclufion of the fcene, when he was carried to the fummit of frenzy, as was the cafe before he expired, he had the power of fummoning himfelf, and rationally

ally anfwering queftions all along, with a diftinct voice, fuch as maniacs exprefs them-felves in, but more or lefs impetuoufly, ac-cording to the degree of fury with which he was agitated when fpoke to.—At the appearance of a lighted fire or candle, he fhrunk back in terror, calling out to remove them from his fight; and when the bed-clothes were adjufted on him, he always complained of being much hurt.

SUNDAY (12th) rolled his eyes without intermiffion; ftartings of the mufcles of the face; voided fome urine of a greenifh hue, turning whitifh when cold; frequent defire to difcharge urine; quantity fmall, and quality as above; confiderable heat, and moifture on his fkin; a very white, thin fur on his tongue; thirfty; pulfe full, and beat about one hundred and twenty-five, or one hundred and thirty in a minute; head-ach; oppreffion, or heat at his ftomach; inclination to vomit, but was afraid to do fo for the obftruction in his throat.—" With

I i " all

" all thefe fymptoms," fays Mr. Bathie,
" the boy fpoke to me fenfibly (on the 12th)
" and in his ordinary tone of voice, as if
" his throat had been quite well.—Two
" bluifh marks remained where he had been
" bit, but the part was healed."

WATER was now offered : as foon as it
touched the fauces, he was thrown into
convulfions—let go the difh—ftarted to his
feet—grafping his throat with both hands—
his face greatly flufhed—and he continued
in a ftate of fuffocation for a minute, when
the fpafm began to yield, and wore off gradually; this was accompanied by a quick
involuntary action of the mufcles of his
face, and with a convulfive motion of the
whole cheft, fimilar to fobbing, but in
quicker paroxifms, and with a peculiar noife
from the throat.—Thirft extreme.—Encreafed in fury and madnefs now, fancying,
in his frenzy, that his friends and attendants were all confpiring againft his life.—
At laft, could fcarcely be held in bed by
three

three or four men.—He, to the laſt, knew his friends when they ſpoke to him—raving and toſſing about when he had anſwered them.—About eight o'clock in the evening, he turned ſuddenly quiet and motionleſs.— He lay in this condition for little more than half an hour, and then expired without a ſtruggle.

From Dr. Berkenhaut's Eſſay on the Bite of a Mad Dog.—Vid. p. 80.

SOME years ago, I was ſent for to attend a young gentleman, in the laſt ſtage of this horrible diſeaſe, who was bit by one of his father's hounds about ſix or ſeven weeks before.—A day or two before I ſaw him, he complained of a pain in the arm which had been bitten, gradually extending towards his ſhoulder. He had taken many doſes of the expreſſed juice of rib-wort, which, in that county, was univerſally deemed a ſpecific, and had bathed every day in the river. I ſaw him about ten in
the

the morning. He complained of nothing
but a pain in his arm, and some little difficulty in swallowing. I ordered a warm
bath to be prepared, in which he sat half
an hour with great composure. I rubbed a
considerable quantity of mercurial ointment
into each arm, and gave him a grain of
crude opium every hour, till nine or ten
o'clock at night, without the least effect.
About eleven, he became extremely rest-
less, and died at twelve, retaining his senses
to the last moment, without any symptoms
of madness, or propensity to bite his attendants.

———————————

Sir Thomas Myerne tells us, dogs are
subject to the following diseases:—1. The
Hot Madness; this, he says, is incurable;
they fly from every thing, and can hold out
but four days.—2. The *Running Madness.*
This is likewise incurable: they fly only
on dogs, and that by fits; and may sometimes, we are told, hold out nine months.
—3. *La Rage Mue*; which is a disease that
lies

lies in the blood.—4. The *Falling Madnefs*;
this feizes on the head, and is a fort of epi-
lepfy.—5. The *Blaſting*, or *Withering*; this
lies in the bowels, which fhrink up exceedingly.—6. The *Sleepy Difeafe*; this, he fays,
comes from little worms in the mouth of
the ftomach —7. The *Rheumatic Difeafe*;
this fwells the head very much, and makes
the eye yellow.—" In thefe five latter dif-
" eafes the dogs will not eat; but they live
" eight or nine days, without hurting any
" body, and then die of hunger."—[Vid.
Philof. Tranfact.]—The reader is left to
form his own remarks on this.

*The following appeared in the Ipfwich
Journal of Feb.* 19, 1785, *in confequence of fome Thoughts on Hydrophobia publifhed therein fome weeks before.*

THE public has been much obliged by
an advertifement in the Ipfwich Journal of
the 5th of this inftant February, advifing
proper care to be taken with dogs likely to
be

be mad; but that part relating to what is commonly called *worming* of dogs to prevent their madnefs, is a miftake, it being done to prevent their biting any thing when mad: experience having fhewn, time out of mind, that by taking out the tendon which grows under the tongue, not one fingle inftance has ever happened of any perfon being bit by a dog fo wormed. And it has been obferved, that out of feveral packs of hounds, and many other dogs that have been mad, thofe wormed have fallen off their meat, refufed water, and always died fullen, or fleepy mad, not one of them ever offering to bite any thing; when other dogs, part of the fame pack of hounds, which were neglected to be wormed, though bit at the fame time by the fame mad dog, have acted as ufual, biting every thing that came in their way.—Whether this tendon under the dog's tongue be, during his madnefs, full of extreme pain, or violent heat, and the caufe of his fnapping at and biting every thing he meets, is hard to determine;

but

but as experience has all along shewn, that taking away this tendon (which is drawn out without the least difficulty) has always prevented biting, &c. why should this preventive precaution ever be neglected?

In reply to the foregoing, the following was inserted in the same Journal, March 5.

A C A R D.

DR. H. presents his compliments to the author of the stricture, inserted in the Ipswich Journal of February 19, relative to the worming of dogs; thanks him for his approbation of the observations on Hydrophobia; fears there may be some misinformation in what is advanced of packs of hounds being so much changed from the common course, when seized with madness, by the extraction of the little tendinous ligament under the tongue.

MAN-

MANKIND have been too apt to follow the traditions of their forefathers, without consulting their own reason and judgement; or have drawn too hasty conclusions from experiments, through neglect of carefully weighing every circumstance.

IT must in the first place be admitted, that an effect can never be greater than its cause. This is a maxim Dr. H. thinks indisputable. The extirpation here contended for, seems very inadequate to the change said to be thereby produced. A philosopher will ever be cautious, if his aim be truth, the encrease of knowledge, and the removal of popular prejudice, or popular error, of assenting to assertions which have not for their basis well instituted experiment, where results have been marked with accuracy, and related with fidelity.

IT appears from the expressions "it has "been observed, that out of several packs of "hounds

" hounds, &c." that the author has not made the experiment himſelf ; therefore, may he not, through a confidence on the veracity and diſcernment of others in diſtinguiſhing phænomena, have ſuffered himſelf to be impoſed on ? If he ſpeaks from authority which he can truſt, his readers ſhould have been referred to it.

THERE appears no reaſon to argue from facts, till once they are well eſtabliſhed, otherwiſe he might be told, that both ten-dons and ligaments, or tendinous-ligaments, as the accurate Morgagni inclines to call this, are endowed with leſs degrees of ſenſibi-lity, than ſofter parts poſſeſſed of more nume-rous nerves, and larger blood veſſels. This is now pretty well eſtabliſhed among phy-ſiologiſts:—This, however, is not meant to deny an encreaſe of ſenſibility to them in a ſtate of diſeaſe ; or that they are incapable of inflammation ; but it is refuſing to admit them more ſenſible, in proportion to other

K k   parts

parts differently furnifhed with organs, that are the medium of fenfibility.

THE pain in the organs of deglutition, occafioned by the fpafms brought on from the virus; the changed ftate of the falival fecretion, and degree of irritation thereby given, are fufficient to account for the dog's change of temper, &c. without having re-courfe to a fuppofed pain, and extraordinary heat, in fo diminutive a part as the fmall tendinous ligament referred to.

THE falling off from their meat; the melancholy and fleepy appearance of dogs infected with madnefs, are always the firft fymptoms. Hydrophobia, or the refufal of water, &c. follows. The power of fnapping, or biting, depends on the motion of the under jaw; if the mufcles, appropriated for this office are thrown into violent and fixed fpafms, called in the human body Trifmus, (locked jaw) the animal cannot bite; the power of opening or fhutting the mouth

no

no longer remains: in the laft hours of a dog's illnefs this has been obferved. Sometimes, likewife, the tongue lolls out before death, no power of biting remaining.

Dogs, which poffefs different conftitutions, in fome meafure analogous to the human race, have alfo a variety in their fymptoms, and muft therefore be differently affected by the fame caufe. The different tempers of dogs prove to a demonftration the different make of their fibres, and form of their various organs, and will fufficiently, it is apprehended, account for all the variety obfervable in the manner of death from madnefs.

All thefe things confidered, it cannot be allowed, without more certain experiment than the fubject has yet undergone, that the taking out this diminutive part has influence enough on the animal to alter his difpofition, or lull fenfibility.

BESIDES

BESIDES, as nature never does any thing in vain, she must have formed this little organ for some useful purpose to the animal. Why then deprive him of it till there be more ample assurance of its having such power over the mind of the animal?

THE limits of a newspaper forbid any farther discussion. Should these remarks not satisfy the gentleman for whom they are thrown out, Dr. H. will chearfully embrace a private correspondence, in order to enter farther into an investigation of the subject; though he confesses it scarcely would seem to deserve it; but must decline any thing farther in a public paper, as being an improper vehicle for such discussions.

The

*The following, however, appeared in the
Ipswich Journal for March 19—it is
suppofed, from the fame anonymous writer.*

For the GOOD of the PUBLIC.

IT has been the received opinion, from
experience, that the alarming mifchief
which frequently happens from the bite of
a mad dog, may be effectually prevented by
worming of all dogs, by taking out the
long tendon, or fibrous mufcle, which
grows under the tongue, and which is
thought to be much fwelled, particularly
inflamed, and the fole caufe of the biting
during the madnefs; thofe dogs that have
been wormed having always died fleepy
mad, never offering to run away from home,
to fnap at, or bite any thing. Many things
may be fully credited, though not eafily to
be accounted for. It will always be prudent to tie up fuch dogs as have been
wormed,

wormed, upon the firſt ſymptoms of madneſs, though moſt people have not even
thought that a neceſſary precaution. The
injury done to the dog is very little indeed,
if any, and not worth mentioning, in com-
pariſon with the fatal conſequences attending the bite of a mad dog. Some people
think it their duty to the public, never to
keep a dog that has not been wormed.

From the ſame Journal of April 16, in reply.

To the PUBLIC.

In the Ipſwich Journal for March 5th,
ſome arguments were adduced with a view
to prove the inutility of worming dogs, to
prevent their biting when affected with
rabies; and doubts were there entertained
relative to the authenticity of ſome ſeeming
facts laid before the public, in order to
eſtabliſh the belief of the ſalutary effects of
this vulgar practice.

PRE-

PREJUDICES inculcated in early youth are ſtrong, and yield with difficulty to reaſon, eſpecially if imbibed from perſons for whom we have an eſteem and veneration. Hence traditions handed down from father to ſon are tenaciouſly held, though they want even the ſemblance of truth to ſupport them.

WE love and venerate our parents; we greedily imbibe their opinions, and conſider them as incontrovertible, without the leaſt doubt but they ſtand ſupported on the firmeſt foundation of facts. Yet, if we do not firſt doubt, and next inveſtigate, it becomes impoſſible ever to advance in improvement, or arrive at a certainty of truth.

HAD not Sir Iſaac Newton doubted that the ſyſtems of former aſtronomers were erroneous, and incapable rationally of explaining various phænomena relative to the heavenly bodies, we never ſhould have been pre-

presented with that system of beauty and simplicity, by which his discoveries have enlightened mankind.—Had not Harvey been a sceptic, we should have yet remained in darkness with respect to the circulation of the blood in animals, and the consequent improvements founded thereon.—And had not later philosophers doubted the truth of Des Cartes' system, and thence exposed it, we might at present still continue in the absurd belief, that the soul could be confined to a small protuberance within the cranium, situated behind the part from whence proceed the optic nerves, called, by anatomists, Pineal Gland, not larger than a common pea.

When we question the truth of opinions, it is by applying them to the test of judgment and reason; and lastly, to confirm this decision, where the case requires it, and the subject will admit, we have recourse to experiment. This is our *ne plus ultra*—it fixes the fate of the investigation. From hence-

henceforth oppofition muft ceafe, and truth becomes triumphant; for to this determination all muft yield. This is the fame, whether the thing to be inveftigated, on which the conteft may turn, be a matter of *great*, or a matter of *fmall* moment, as happens in the prefent.

To come, then, to the point. Dr. James, and others, doubted the utility of the practice mentioned at the beginning of this article; but they produced no experiments to oppofe the error, and confirm the juftnefs of their doubts. The writer of this article doubted likewife, from the apparent abfurdity of the thing, and the difproportion between the caufe and the effect faid to be produced. He had, however, no experiment then, on which he could abfolutely reft; his proofs, therefore, were built on reafoning—were prefumptive only—not pofitive. But, not altogether fatisfied with this, he wifhed to trace it farther, and arrive, if poffible, at certainty. He has at

L l   length

length fortunately fucceeded to his wifh, as the following relation will amply teftify; where experience convinces, that wormed dogs are not incapable of biting when mad; nor do they always die fullen.

A PERSON of veracity in Ipfwich, who practifes worming of dogs, declares, that many of thofe he wormed have gone mad. But he relates, and is ready, when called on, to atteft, that, among others, he wormed a dog for one Cutting, a butcher, of this town (Ipfwich). That the dog not only went mad, but bit a cow, a gander, and a fpaniel of his own, on which he fet great value. The cow and the gander, foon after, likewife went mad; and to prevent the fame event in his own dog, he fhot him; and adds, that the lofs gave him great un-eafinefs. At another time, two dogs he had wormed alfo went mad, and both ran away, as did the former; but he cannot affert whether they bit other animals. The fame perfon alfo wormed another dog, when

when a puppy of four months old; he remained well till about three years after, *i. e.* till about three months ago, when he went mad, ran away from his mafter, and bit a great number of other dogs, feveral of which went mad foon after. All this can be attefted by different people here; and, fhould any of the readers of this doubt its authenticity, every fatisfaction relative to the affair, that can be required, may be had by applying to the printers of this paper.

HERE, then, are facts, where no error in obfervation can be admitted. This relation was given by the perfon who wormed them, before feveral refpectable witneffes, not long ago, who were then converfing on the fubject; one of whom, fome time after, mentioned it to the writer; on which he fent for the perfon, and had it farther confirmed from his own mouth.

THE readers of this Journal, it is hoped, will excufe the author of this article for

em-

employing fo much of their time on an affair of fo little importance. But it has been productive of the removal of an error; and fo far it has fome utility. Nor will humanity, he thinks, blufh at being the inftrument of preventing an unneceffary practice, giving a degree of pain, without any good purpofe, to a fpecies of animals, whofe fidelity, and attachment to man, claim, in a ftrong degree, his mutual affection and fympathy. Hitherto, however, they had the apology of a fuppofed good to plead. But henceforth there can remain none.—Befides, we are not fenfible of the injury we do the animal by thus mutilating him, and deftroying parts which nature formed not in vain. It is not enough that we may be yet ignorant of its ufe; for, fome purpofe it muft unqueftionably ferve, otherwife the Creator would never have endowed them with an ufelefs organ.   **H.**

July.

July 30, 1785.

MR. RIPSHAW now informs me, that he has learned the fate of two other dogs he wormed; which, as farther proofs to eftablifh the inutility and abfurdity of the practice, we fhall lay before our readers.

ONE of thefe was the property of a Mr. Clubbe, a baker, in this town : he wormed this dog when he was a puppy. About fix months from the date of this, *i. e.* about three years after he was wormed, he became affected, and bit feveral dogs; next day he left his mafter and ran away. Two of the dogs he bit, about three weeks after, went mad : one of thefe belonged to a Mr May-hew, a farmer, at Whitton, a village about two miles from Ipfwich; the other to a gentleman at Bramford, about four miles diftant.—Thefe are facts, and can be well attefted.

I WOULD

I would obferve here, that dogs do not *always* refufe water in madnefs.—The Rev. Mr. Mills, near Boxford, in Suffolk, affured me lately, that his own obfervations enabled him to confirm this remark; and related an inftance, where one of his dogs that went mad, lapped water only a few hours before it died. He added, it lapped with eafe; nor did it fhew a defire to bite, unlefs a ftick was held to it, when it immediately fnapped at it. It fawned on him, likewife as ufual. He took notice, however, of a particular fiercenefs and wildnefs in its eyes, and that it bounded rather than ran.

Mr. Tuson, Surgeon, at Boxford, who was then in company, related a cafe, fimilar in almoft every refpect, which fell within his own knowledge.—Hence the danger in pronouncing a dog *not mad*, becaufe he either laps water, or fawns on his mafter.

To

To conclude thefe remarks, I fhall prefent my readers with the opinion of the late
Dr. Gregory, Profeffor of Medicine in the
Univerfity of Edinburgh, relative to the
production of Hydrophobia.—Speaking of
ftimuli, which, he thinks, are the chief caufe
of the evacuation of the *vefica urinaria*, he
fays,—" You may take it for a general rule,
" that thofe creatures that feed upon animal
" food have their bladder more mufcular,
" and confiderably ftronger, and lefs capa-
" cious, than thofe that live on vegetables,
" fuch as horfes, cows, fwine, &c. whofe
" bladder of urine is perfectly membranous,
" and very large. This is wifely adapted
" to the nature of their food; for, in thefe
" firft, *all their juices are more acrid*; fo, in
" a particular manner, their urine becomes
" exalted, which, as its remora might be
" of very ill confequence, muft neceffarily
" be quickly expelled. This is chiefly ef-
" fected by its ftimulating this vifcus more
" ftrongly to contract, and fo difcharge its
" contents.

" contents.—And if these creatures, whose
" fluids have already a tendency to putri-
" faction, are exposed to heat or hunger,
" the liquids must, for a considerable time,
" undergo the actions of the containing
" vessels, and frequently perform the course
" of the circulation without any new sup-
" plies of food; by which the fluids become
" more and more acrid, the creature is apt
" to fall into *feverish* and *putrid diseases;*
" and, in fact, we find, that *these causes are*
" *sufficient* to produce that fatal and melan-
" choly distemper, the *Rabies Canina, Vul-*
" *pina,* &c. in these animals: whereas
" those that feed on vegetable food seldom
" or never contract those diseases, but by
" infection."—Vid. Essay on Comparative
Anatomy.

In page 69 we promised to lay before
our readers the noted powder of Palmerius;
" Whose power he believes sufficient to be
" trusted with operating a cure, even though
" the patient should neglect all due treat-
" ment

" ment of his wound, or obfervation of
" regimen in diet; and to be able, not
" only to work a prophylactic, or prevent-
" ative cure, but likewife a radical cure of
" the Hydrophobia already prefent."—The
prefcription is as follows:

" TAKE of the leaves of rue, vervain,
" fage of virtue, plaintain, (and polypody
" leaves) common wormwood, mint, mug-
" wort, baum, betony, St. John's-wort,
" and of the leffer centaury, each equal
" parts by weight."

WHEN thefe were to be ufed, they were
to be reduced feparately into a fine powder
a dram of which was to be adminiftered
daily to the bitten patient, mixed with twice
as much fugar, in a draught of wine, or
cyder, or broth; or made into an electuary
with honey, to be fwallowed on a fafting
ftomach, three hours before taking food.

F I N I S.

ERRATA.

p. 3. l. 9, for them, read *it*. p. 8. l. 3. for fuperfluous, read *fuperfluous*. p. 40. l. 9. for Henry II. read *Forefter of Henry II*. p. 101. l. 6. after urine, add *in*. p. 131. note l. 5. for ut pote, read *utpote*. p. 181. l. 5. from bottom, for were, read *was*. p. 193. l. 10. for evening read *night*. *ibid*. l. 5. from bottom, after became more and more, add *violent*. p. 212. l. 3. after means, add *commonly*. p. 214. l. 10. dele *is*. p. 216. l. 13. for days, read *weeks*.

www.ingramcontent.com/pod-product-compliance
Lightning Source LLC
Chambersburg PA
CBHW060607030726
47498CB00005B/1574